Secret Smithsonian Adventures

THE WRONG WRIGHTS

CHRIS KIENTZ

STEVE HOCKENSMITH

LEE NIELSEN

SMITHSONIAN BOOKS

WASHINGTON

Secret Smithsonian Adventures

THE WRONG WRIGHTS

Story by
Steve Hockensmith and Chris Kientz

Illustration by
Lee Nielsen

Color by
Lee Nielsen

Assistant Colorist
Keil Hunka

Lettering by
Dalaney LaGrange

Original Research by
Anthony Bellotti

This book may be purchased for educational, business, or sales promotional use.
For information, please write: Special Markets Department,
Smithsonian Books, P. O. Box 37012, MRC 513, Washington, DC 20013

Published by Smithsonian Books
Director: Carolyn Gleason
Production Editor: Christina Wiginton

Library of Congress Cataloging-in-Publication Data is available upon request.
Manufactured in the United States of America
20 19 18 17 16   5 4 3 2 1

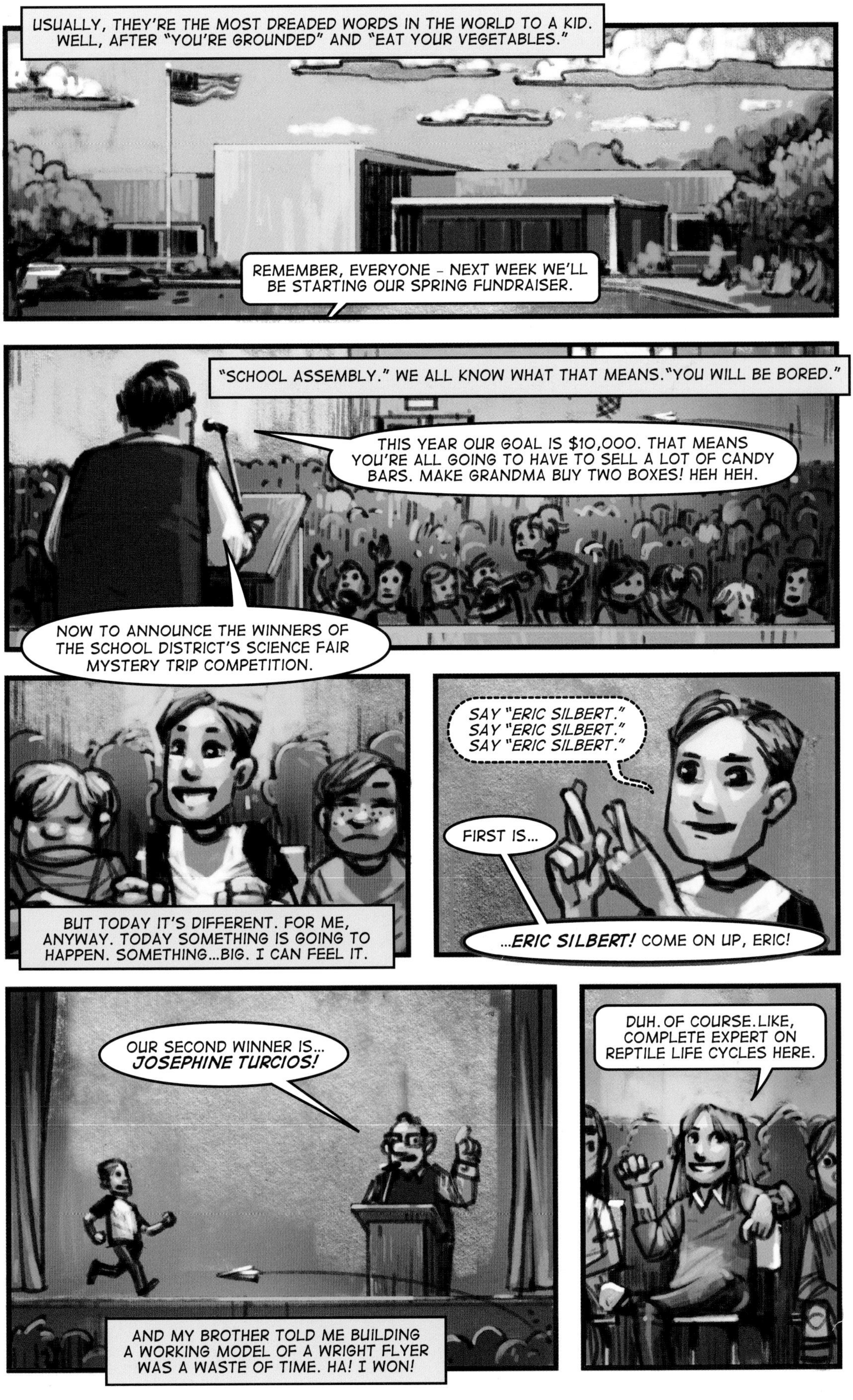
USUALLY, THEY'RE THE MOST DREADED WORDS IN THE WORLD TO A KID. WELL, AFTER "YOU'RE GROUNDED" AND "EAT YOUR VEGETABLES."
REMEMBER, EVERYONE - NEXT WEEK WE'LL BE STARTING OUR SPRING FUNDRAISER.
"SCHOOL ASSEMBLY." WE ALL KNOW WHAT THAT MEANS. "YOU WILL BE BORED."
THIS YEAR OUR GOAL IS $10,000. THAT MEANS YOU'RE ALL GOING TO HAVE TO SELL A LOT OF CANDY BARS. MAKE GRANDMA BUY TWO BOXES! HEH HEH.
NOW TO ANNOUNCE THE WINNERS OF THE SCHOOL DISTRICT'S SCIENCE FAIR MYSTERY TRIP COMPETITION.
BUT TODAY IT'S DIFFERENT. FOR ME, ANYWAY. TODAY SOMETHING IS GOING TO HAPPEN. SOMETHING...BIG. I CAN FEEL IT.
SAY "ERIC SILBERT." SAY "ERIC SILBERT." SAY "ERIC SILBERT."
FIRST IS...
...*ERIC SILBERT!* COME ON UP, ERIC!
OUR SECOND WINNER IS... *JOSEPHINE TURCIOS!*
AND MY BROTHER TOLD ME BUILDING A WORKING MODEL OF A WRIGHT FLYER WAS A WASTE OF TIME. HA! I WON!
DUH. OF COURSE. LIKE, COMPLETE EXPERT ON REPTILE LIFE CYCLES HERE.

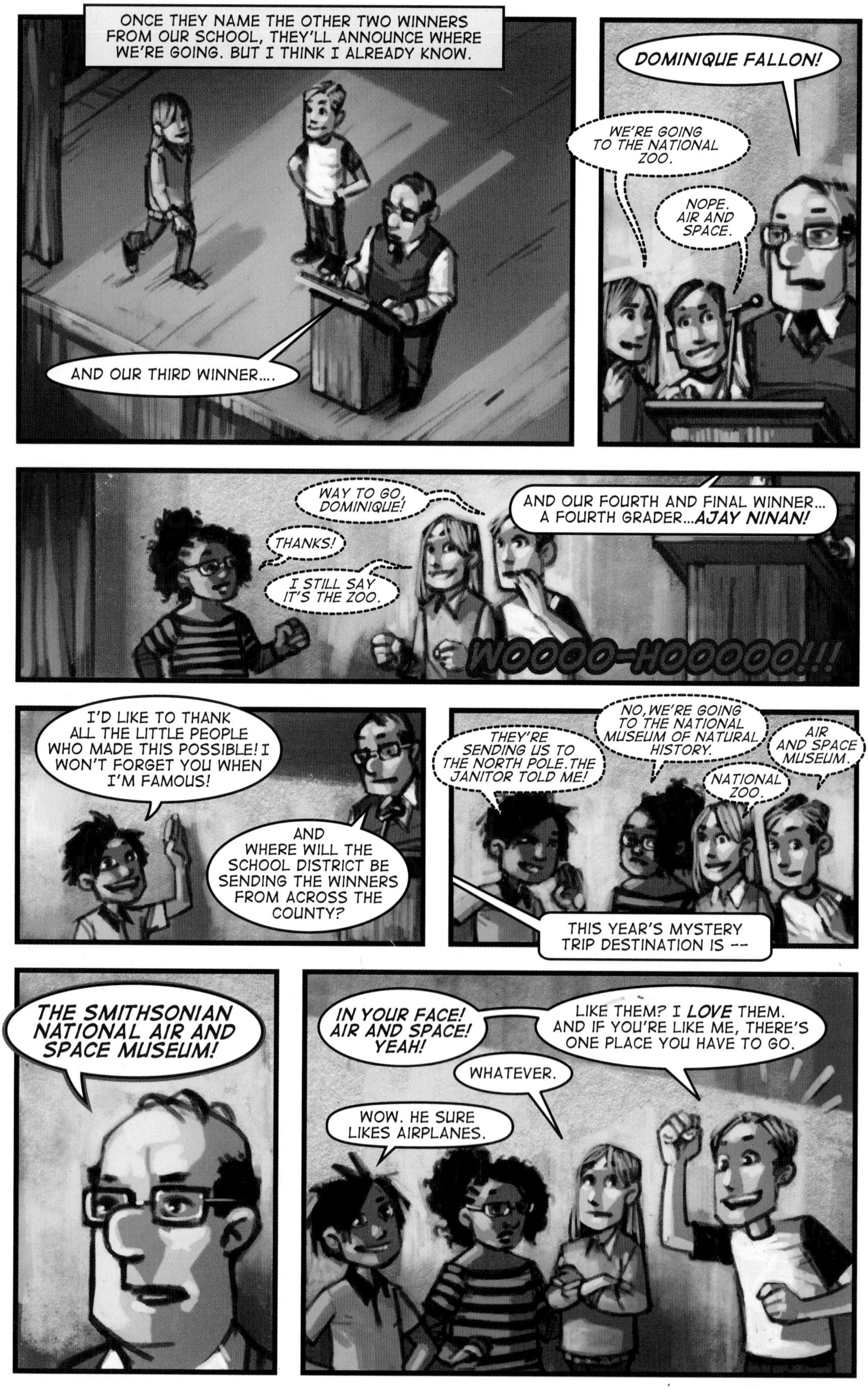
ONCE THEY NAME THE OTHER TWO WINNERS FROM OUR SCHOOL, THEY'LL ANNOUNCE WHERE WE'RE GOING. BUT I THINK I ALREADY KNOW.
AND OUR THIRD WINNER....
DOMINIQUE FALLON!
WE'RE GOING TO THE NATIONAL ZOO.
NOPE. AIR AND SPACE.
WAY TO GO, DOMINIQUE!
THANKS!
I STILL SAY IT'S THE ZOO.
AND OUR FOURTH AND FINAL WINNER... A FOURTH GRADER...AJAY NINAN!
WOOOO-HOOOOO!!!
I'D LIKE TO THANK ALL THE LITTLE PEOPLE WHO MADE THIS POSSIBLE! I WON'T FORGET YOU WHEN I'M FAMOUS!
AND WHERE WILL THE SCHOOL DISTRICT BE SENDING THE WINNERS FROM ACROSS THE COUNTY?
THEY'RE SENDING US TO THE NORTH POLE.THE JANITOR TOLD ME!
NO,WE'RE GOING TO THE NATIONAL MUSEUM OF NATURAL HISTORY.
AIR AND SPACE MUSEUM.
NATIONAL ZOO.
THIS YEAR'S MYSTERY TRIP DESTINATION IS --
THE SMITHSONIAN NATIONAL AIR AND SPACE MUSEUM!
IN YOUR FACE! AIR AND SPACE! YEAH!
LIKE THEM? I LOVE THEM. AND IF YOU'RE LIKE ME, THERE'S ONE PLACE YOU HAVE TO GO.
WHATEVER.
WOW. HE SURE LIKES AIRPLANES.

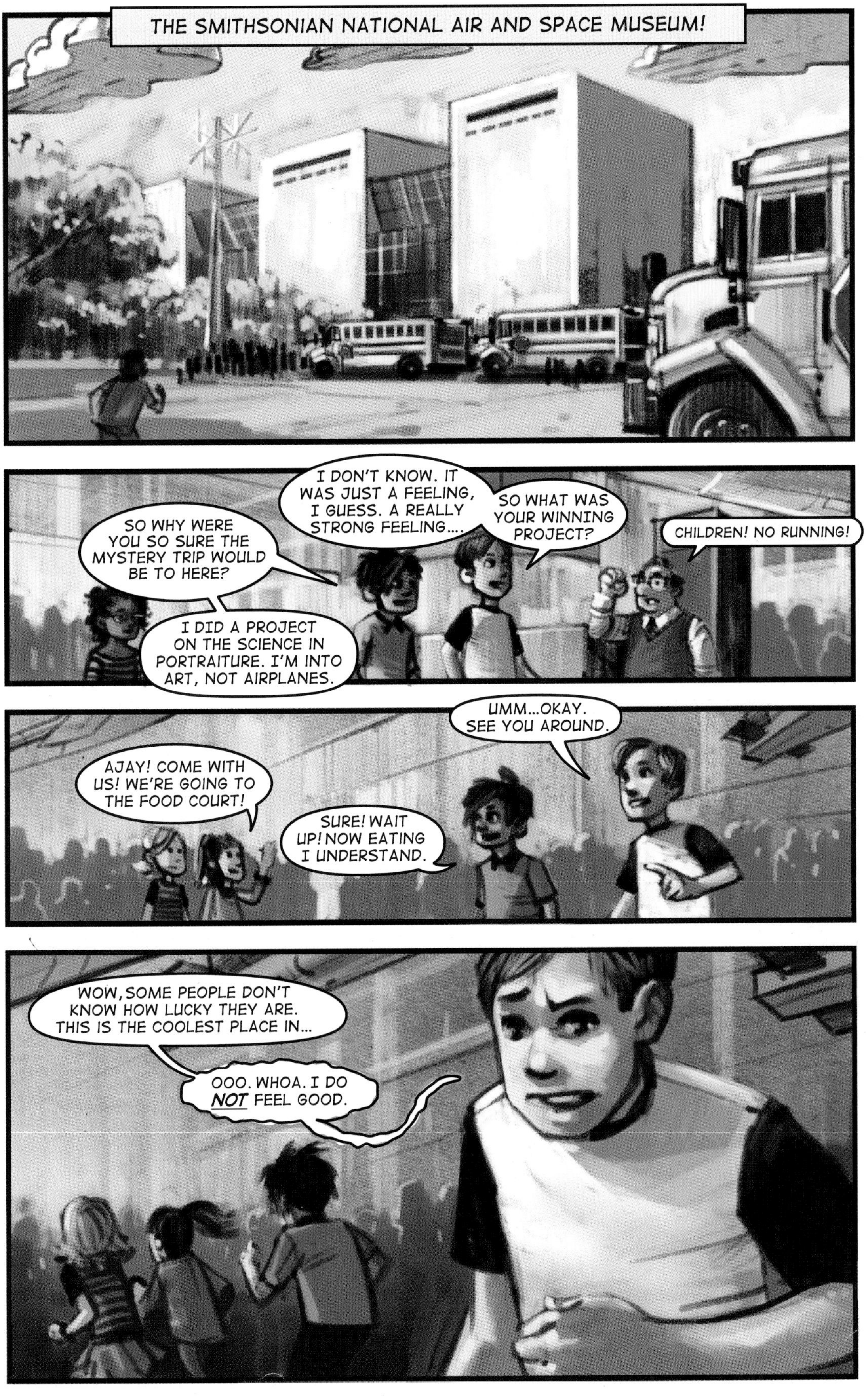
THE SMITHSONIAN NATIONAL AIR AND SPACE MUSEUM!
SO WHY WERE YOU SO SURE THE MYSTERY TRIP WOULD BE TO HERE?
I DON'T KNOW. IT WAS JUST A FEELING, I GUESS. A REALLY STRONG FEELING....
SO WHAT WAS YOUR WINNING PROJECT?
I DID A PROJECT ON THE SCIENCE IN PORTRAITURE. I'M INTO ART, NOT AIRPLANES.
CHILDREN! NO RUNNING!
AJAY! COME WITH US! WE'RE GOING TO THE FOOD COURT!
SURE! WAIT UP! NOW EATING I UNDERSTAND.
UMM...OKAY. SEE YOU AROUND.
WOW, SOME PEOPLE DON'T KNOW HOW LUCKY THEY ARE. THIS IS THE COOLEST PLACE IN...
OOO. WHOA. I DO **NOT** FEEL GOOD.

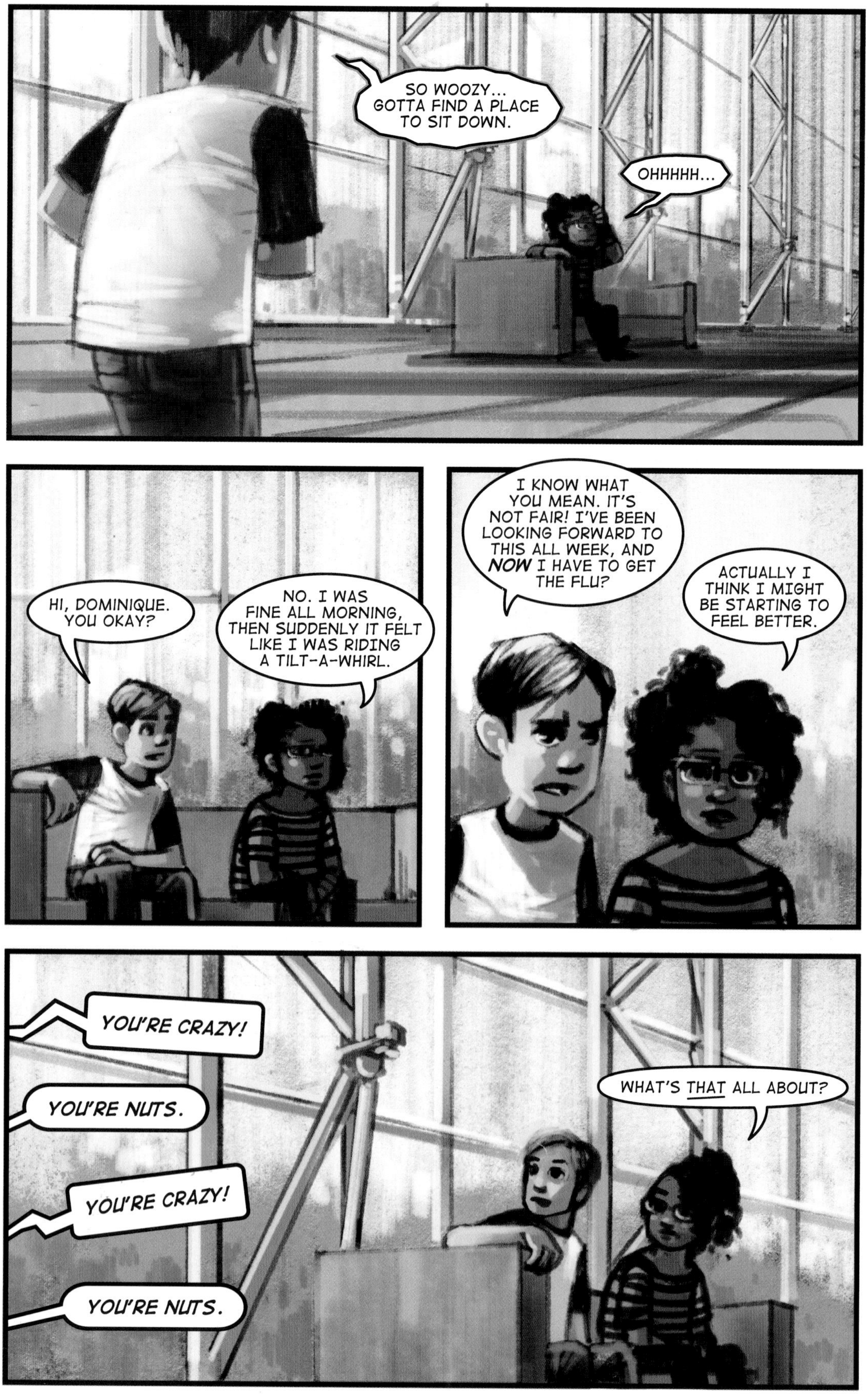
SO WOOZY... GOTTA FIND A PLACE TO SIT DOWN.
OHHHHH...
HI, DOMINIQUE. YOU OKAY?
NO. I WAS FINE ALL MORNING, THEN SUDDENLY IT FELT LIKE I WAS RIDING A TILT-A-WHIRL.
I KNOW WHAT YOU MEAN. IT'S NOT FAIR! I'VE BEEN LOOKING FORWARD TO THIS ALL WEEK, AND NOW I HAVE TO GET THE FLU?
ACTUALLY I THINK I MIGHT BE STARTING TO FEEL BETTER.
YOU'RE CRAZY!
YOU'RE NUTS.
YOU'RE CRAZY!
YOU'RE NUTS.
WHAT'S THAT ALL ABOUT?

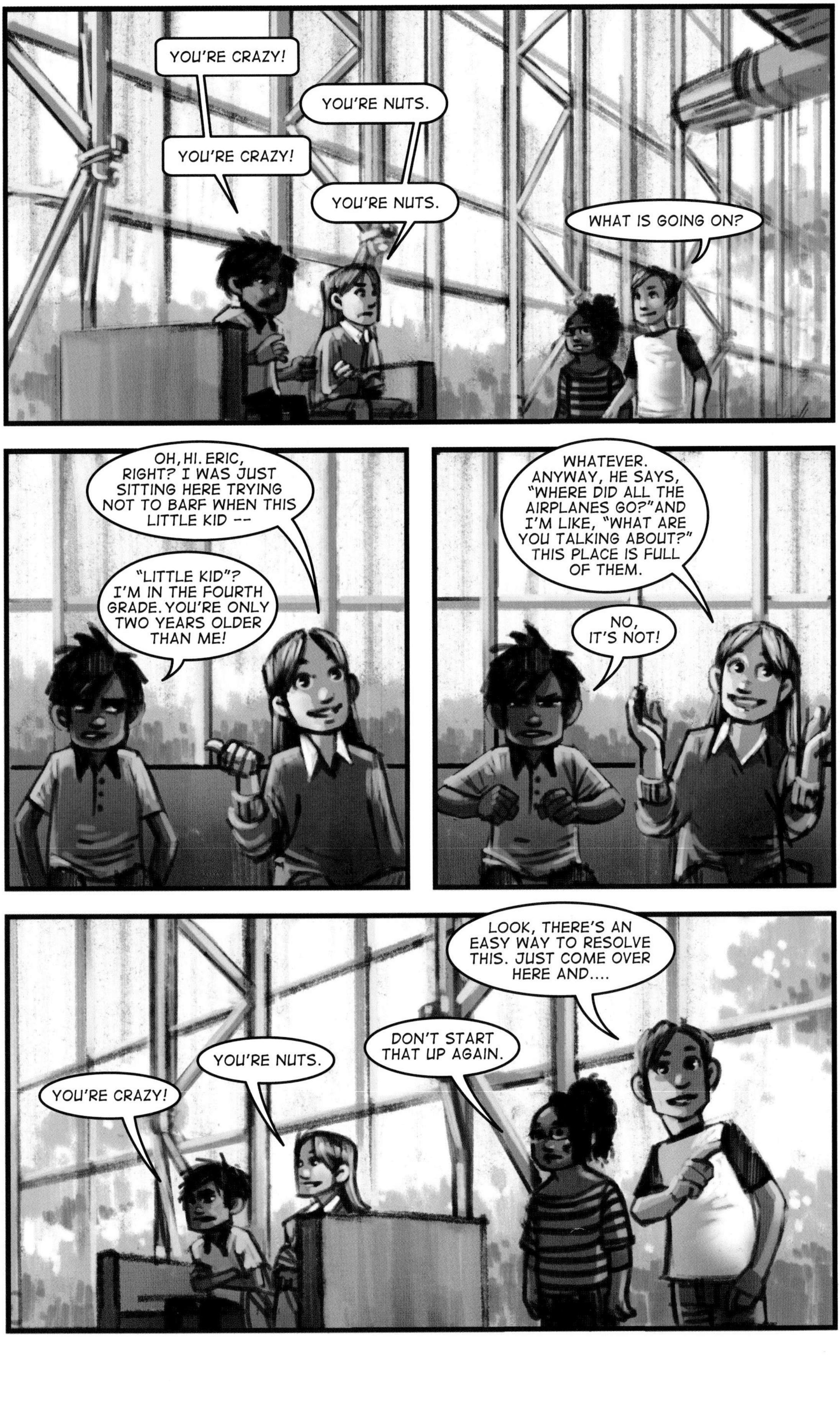
YOU'RE CRAZY!
YOU'RE NUTS.
YOU'RE CRAZY!
YOU'RE NUTS.
WHAT IS GOING ON?
OH, HI. ERIC, RIGHT? I WAS JUST SITTING HERE TRYING NOT TO BARF WHEN THIS LITTLE KID --
"LITTLE KID"? I'M IN THE FOURTH GRADE. YOU'RE ONLY TWO YEARS OLDER THAN ME!
WHATEVER. ANYWAY, HE SAYS, "WHERE DID ALL THE AIRPLANES GO?" AND I'M LIKE, "WHAT ARE YOU TALKING ABOUT?" THIS PLACE IS FULL OF THEM.
NO, IT'S NOT!
YOU'RE CRAZY!
YOU'RE NUTS.
DON'T START THAT UP AGAIN.
LOOK, THERE'S AN EASY WAY TO RESOLVE THIS. JUST COME OVER HERE AND....

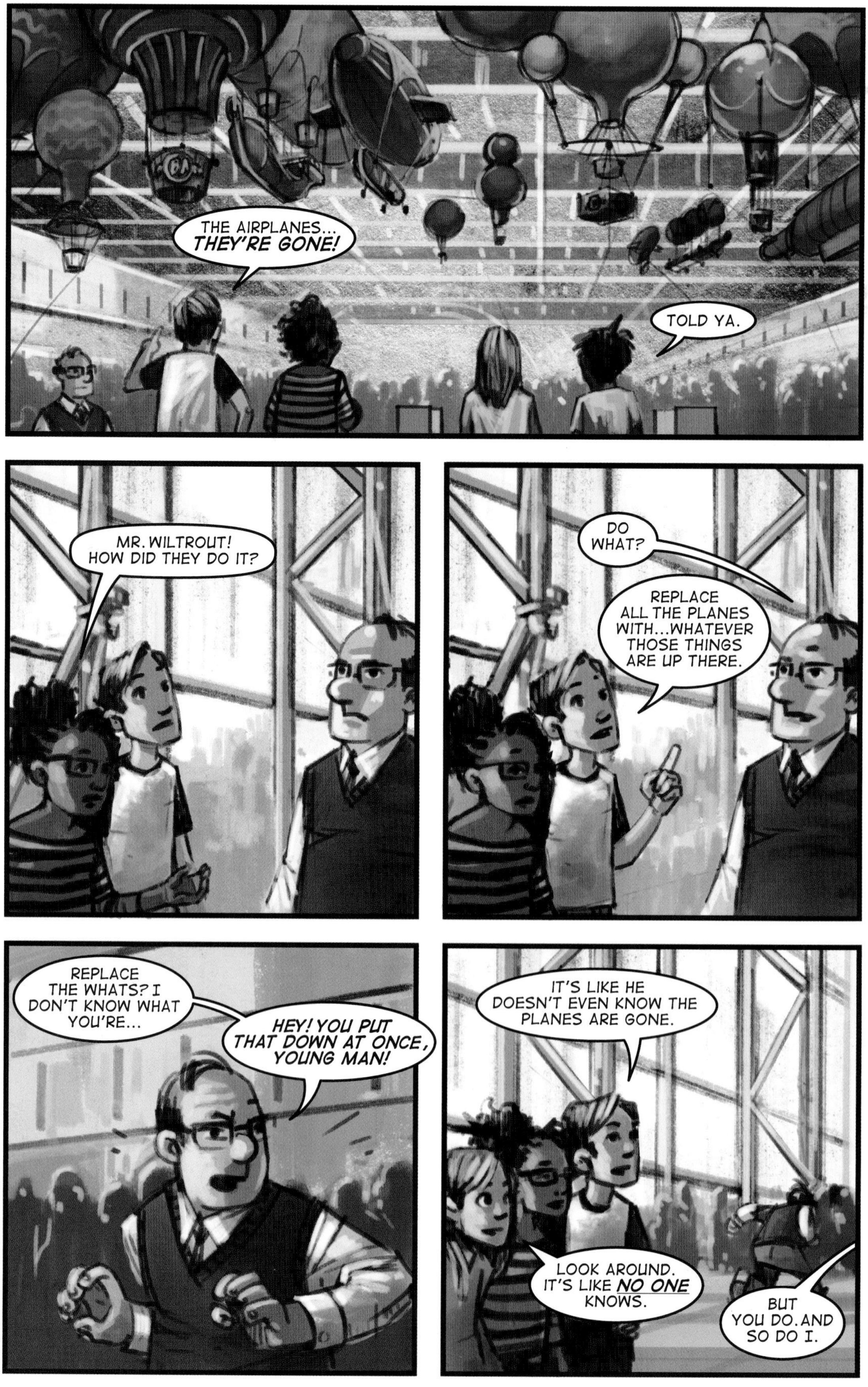
THE AIRPLANES... THEY'RE GONE!
TOLD YA.
MR. WILTROUT! HOW DID THEY DO IT?
DO WHAT?
REPLACE ALL THE PLANES WITH...WHATEVER THOSE THINGS ARE UP THERE.
REPLACE THE WHATS? I DON'T KNOW WHAT YOU'RE...
HEY! YOU PUT THAT DOWN AT ONCE, YOUNG MAN!
IT'S LIKE HE DOESN'T EVEN KNOW THE PLANES ARE GONE.
LOOK AROUND. IT'S LIKE NO ONE KNOWS.
BUT YOU DO. AND SO DO I.

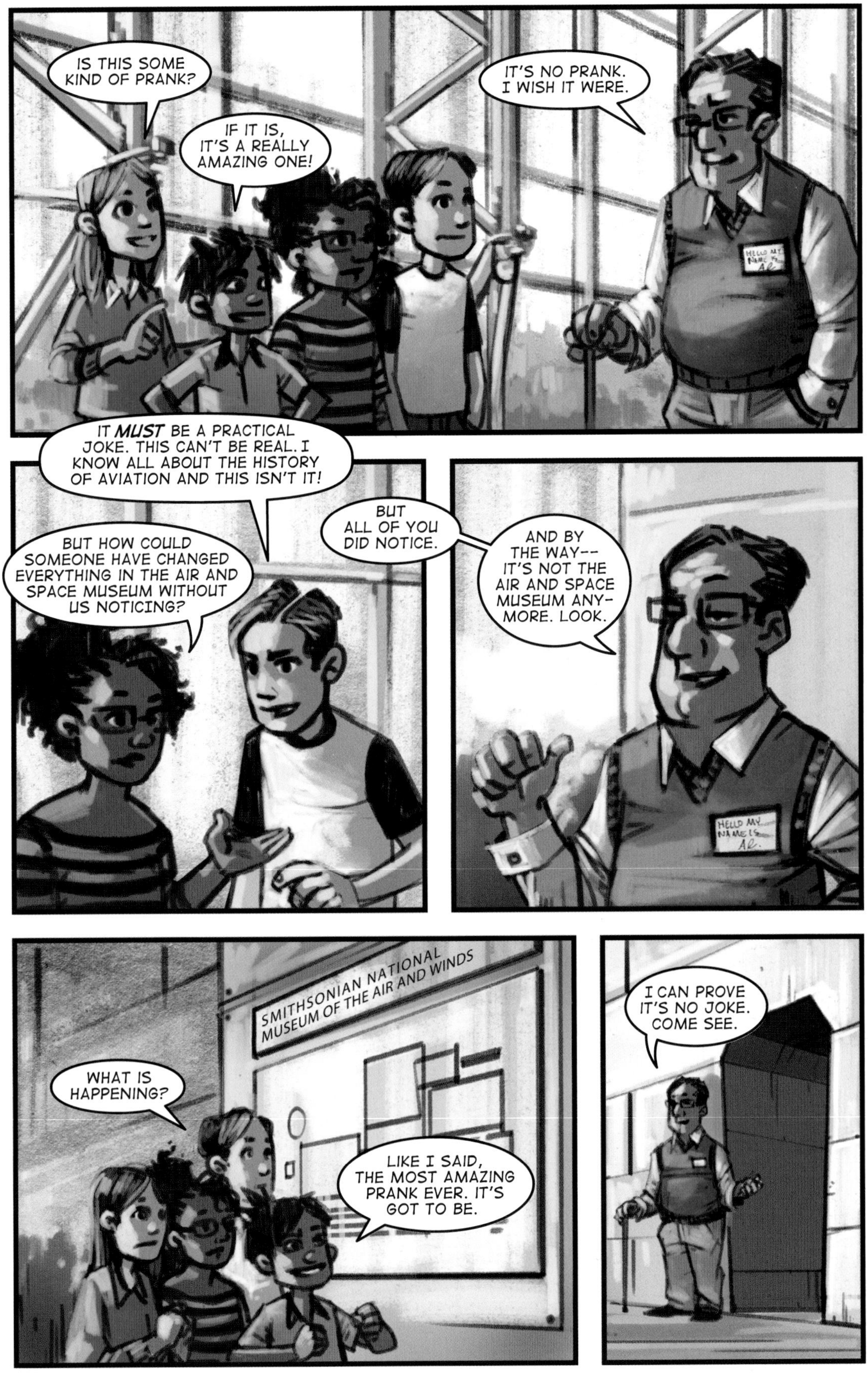
IS THIS SOME KIND OF PRANK?
IF IT IS, IT'S A REALLY AMAZING ONE!
IT'S NO PRANK. I WISH IT WERE.
HELLO MY NAME IS AL
IT **MUST** BE A PRACTICAL JOKE. THIS CAN'T BE REAL. I KNOW ALL ABOUT THE HISTORY OF AVIATION AND THIS ISN'T IT!
BUT HOW COULD SOMEONE HAVE CHANGED EVERYTHING IN THE AIR AND SPACE MUSEUM WITHOUT US NOTICING?
BUT ALL OF YOU DID NOTICE.
AND BY THE WAY-- IT'S NOT THE AIR AND SPACE MUSEUM ANY- MORE. LOOK.
HELLO MY NAME IS AL
SMITHSONIAN NATIONAL MUSEUM OF THE AIR AND WINDS
WHAT IS HAPPENING?
LIKE I SAID, THE MOST AMAZING PRANK EVER. IT'S GOT TO BE.
I CAN PROVE IT'S NO JOKE. COME SEE.

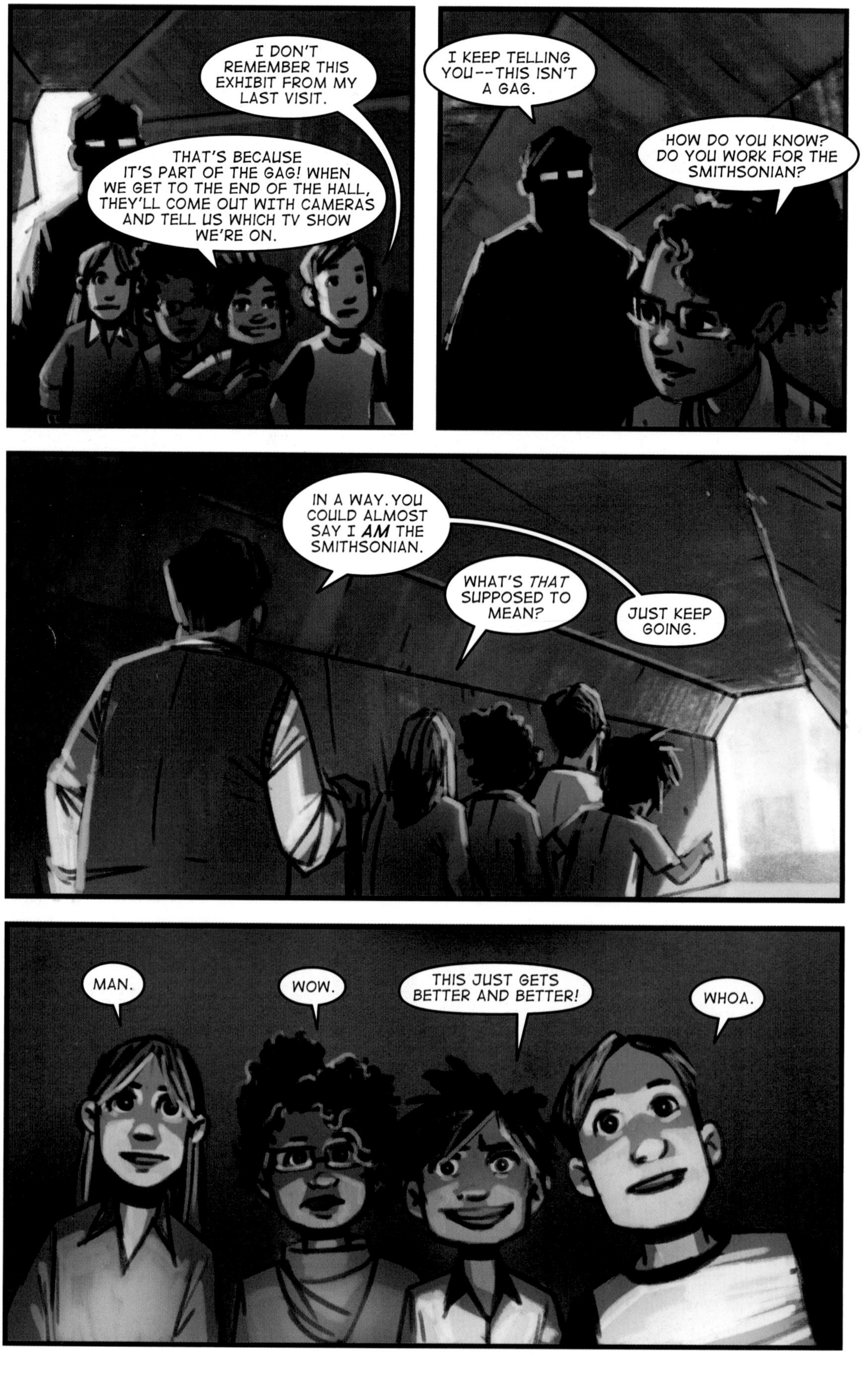
I DON'T REMEMBER THIS EXHIBIT FROM MY LAST VISIT.
THAT'S BECAUSE IT'S PART OF THE GAG! WHEN WE GET TO THE END OF THE HALL, THEY'LL COME OUT WITH CAMERAS AND TELL US WHICH TV SHOW WE'RE ON.
I KEEP TELLING YOU--THIS ISN'T A GAG.
HOW DO YOU KNOW? DO YOU WORK FOR THE SMITHSONIAN?
IN A WAY. YOU COULD ALMOST SAY I AM THE SMITHSONIAN.
WHAT'S THAT SUPPOSED TO MEAN?
JUST KEEP GOING.
MAN.
WOW.
THIS JUST GETS BETTER AND BETTER!
WHOA.

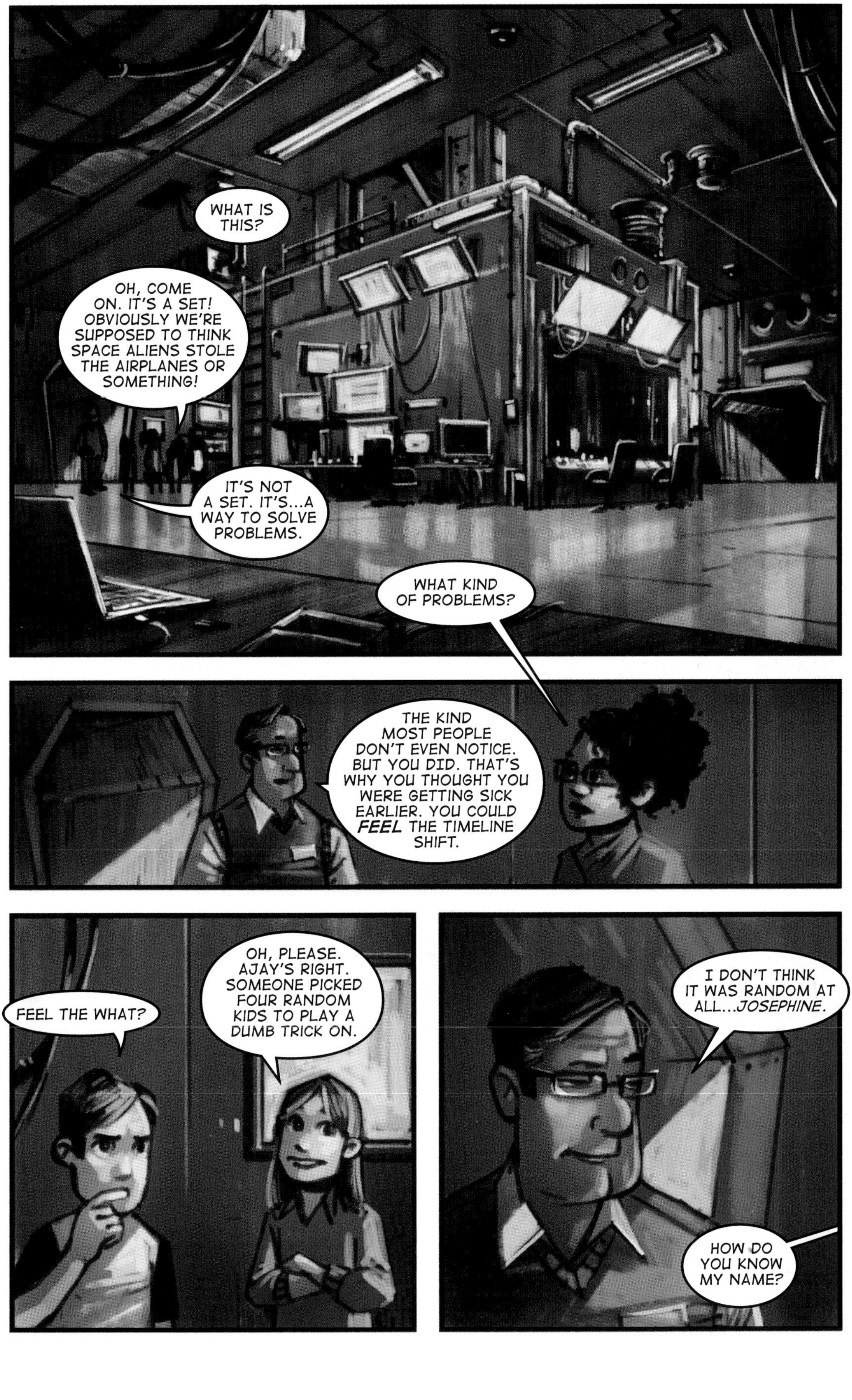
WHAT IS THIS?
OH, COME ON. IT'S A SET! OBVIOUSLY WE'RE SUPPOSED TO THINK SPACE ALIENS STOLE THE AIRPLANES OR SOMETHING!
IT'S NOT A SET. IT'S...A WAY TO SOLVE PROBLEMS.
WHAT KIND OF PROBLEMS?
THE KIND MOST PEOPLE DON'T EVEN NOTICE. BUT YOU DID. THAT'S WHY YOU THOUGHT YOU WERE GETTING SICK EARLIER. YOU COULD *FEEL* THE TIMELINE SHIFT.
FEEL THE WHAT?
OH, PLEASE. AJAY'S RIGHT. SOMEONE PICKED FOUR RANDOM KIDS TO PLAY A DUMB TRICK ON.
I DON'T THINK IT WAS RANDOM AT ALL...*JOSEPHINE*.
HOW DO YOU KNOW MY NAME?

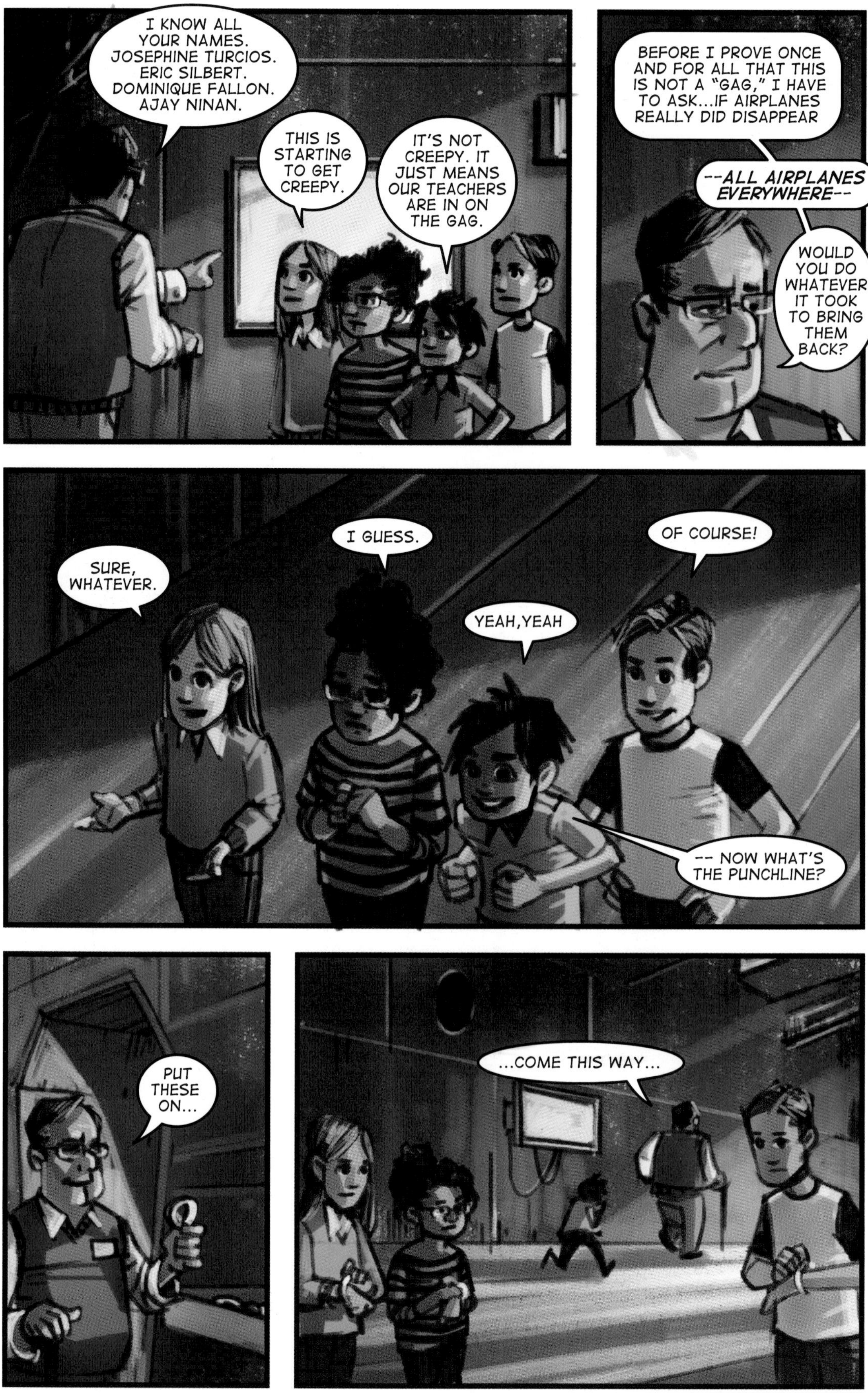
I KNOW ALL YOUR NAMES. JOSEPHINE TURCIOS. ERIC SILBERT. DOMINIQUE FALLON. AJAY NINAN.
THIS IS STARTING TO GET CREEPY.
IT'S NOT CREEPY. IT JUST MEANS OUR TEACHERS ARE IN ON THE GAG.
BEFORE I PROVE ONCE AND FOR ALL THAT THIS IS NOT A "GAG," I HAVE TO ASK...IF AIRPLANES REALLY DID DISAPPEAR
--ALL AIRPLANES EVERYWHERE--
WOULD YOU DO WHATEVER IT TOOK TO BRING THEM BACK?
SURE, WHATEVER.
I GUESS.
YEAH,YEAH
OF COURSE!
-- NOW WHAT'S THE PUNCHLINE?
PUT THESE ON...
...COME THIS WAY...

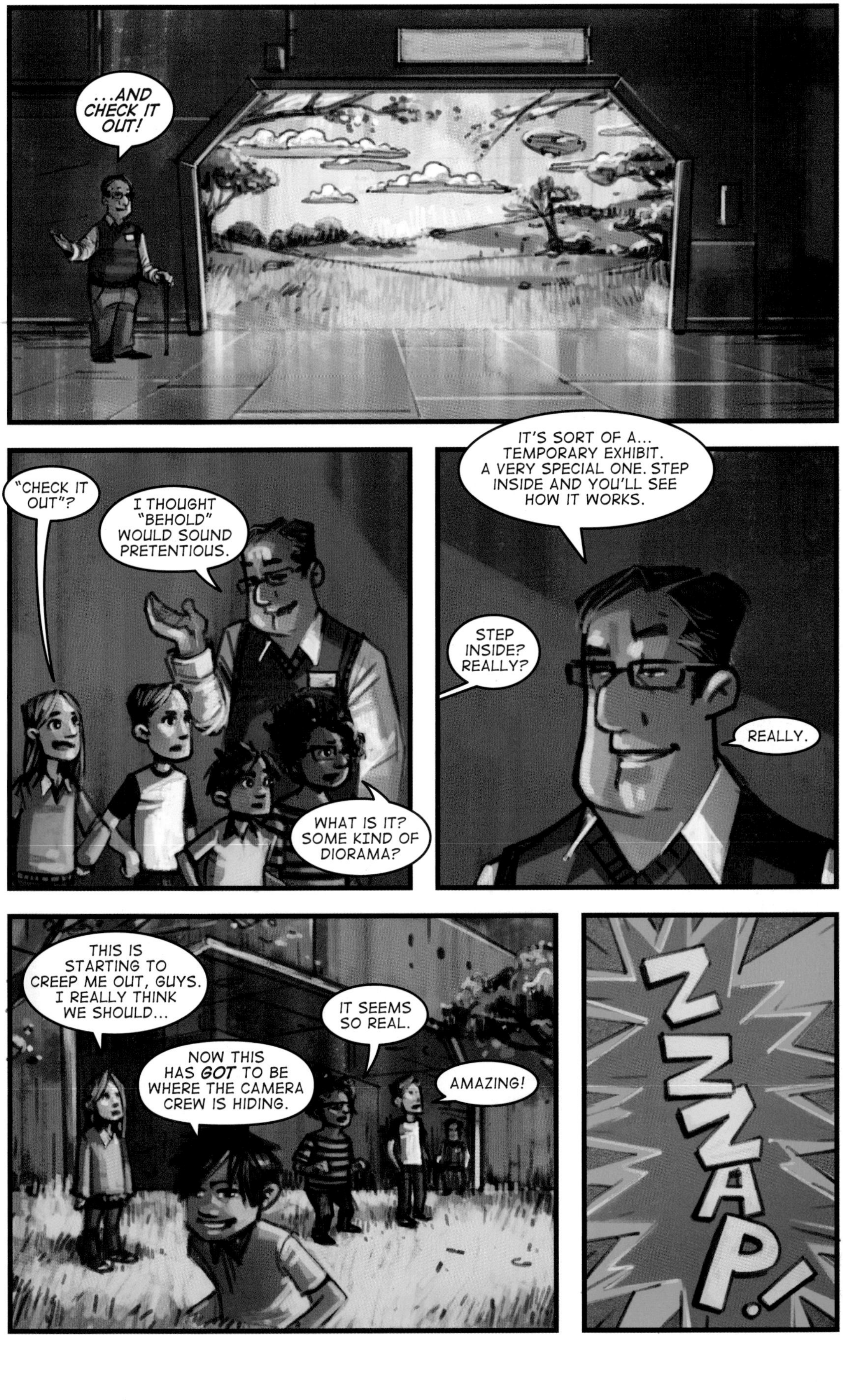
...AND CHECK IT OUT!
"CHECK IT OUT"?
I THOUGHT "BEHOLD" WOULD SOUND PRETENTIOUS.
WHAT IS IT? SOME KIND OF DIORAMA?
IT'S SORT OF A... TEMPORARY EXHIBIT. A VERY SPECIAL ONE. STEP INSIDE AND YOU'LL SEE HOW IT WORKS.
STEP INSIDE? REALLY?
REALLY.
THIS IS STARTING TO CREEP ME OUT, GUYS. I REALLY THINK WE SHOULD...
IT SEEMS SO REAL.
NOW THIS HAS GOT TO BE WHERE THE CAMERA CREW IS HIDING.
AMAZING!
ZZZAP!

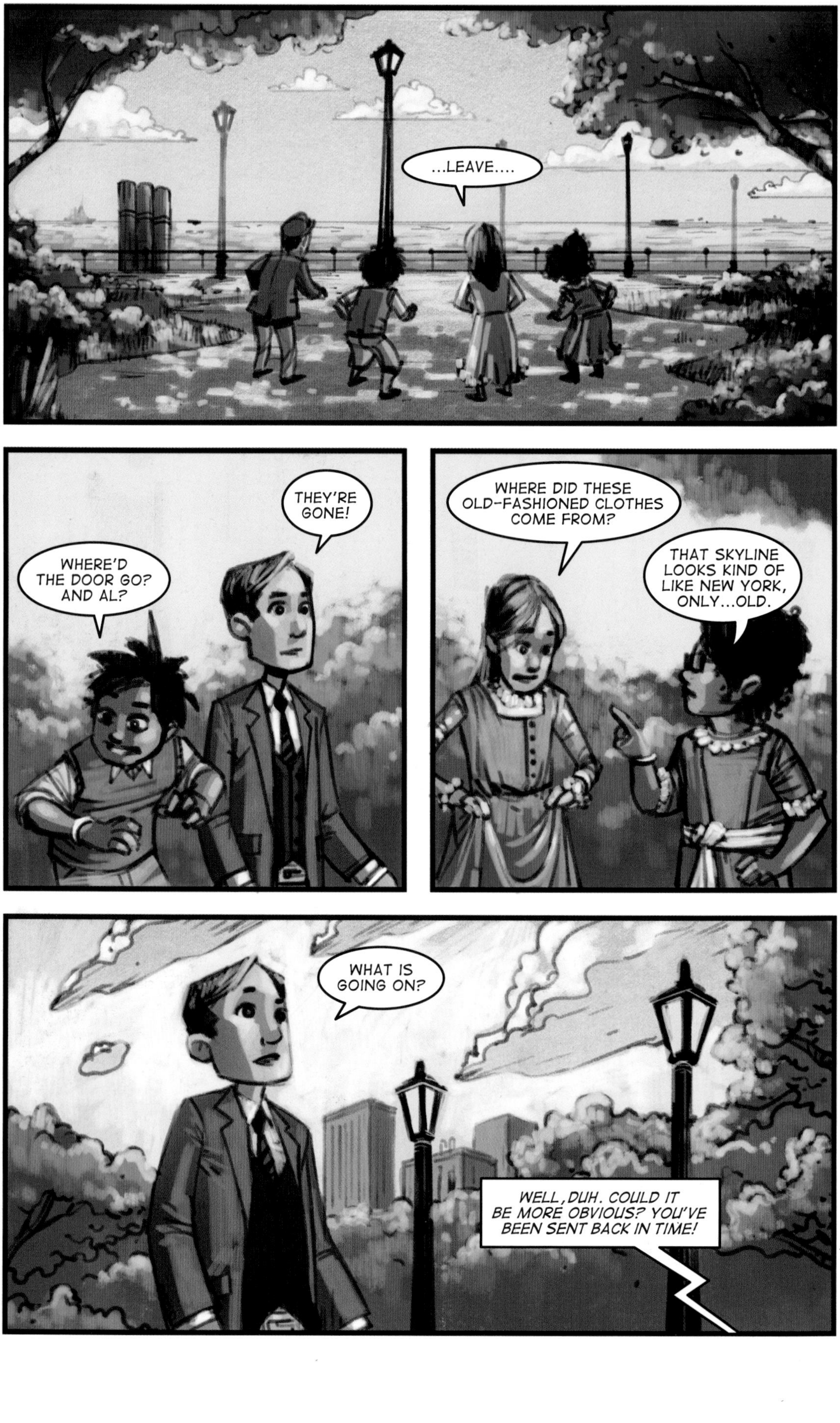
...LEAVE....
THEY'RE GONE!
WHERE'D THE DOOR GO? AND AL?
WHERE DID THESE OLD-FASHIONED CLOTHES COME FROM?
THAT SKYLINE LOOKS KIND OF LIKE NEW YORK, ONLY...OLD.
WHAT IS GOING ON?
WELL, DUH. COULD IT BE MORE OBVIOUS? YOU'VE BEEN SENT BACK IN TIME!

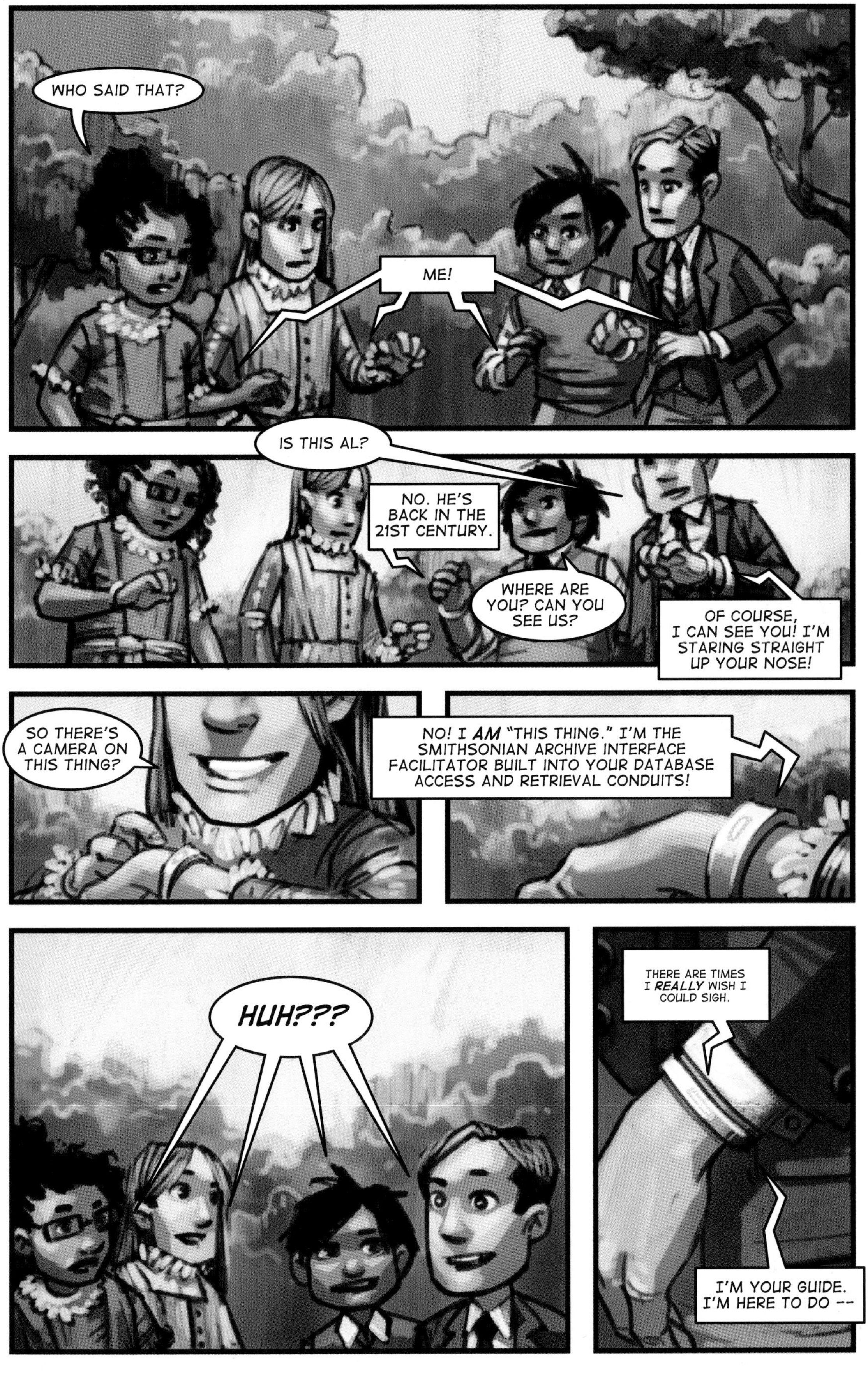
WHO SAID THAT?
ME!
IS THIS AL?
NO. HE'S BACK IN THE 21ST CENTURY.
WHERE ARE YOU? CAN YOU SEE US?
OF COURSE, I CAN SEE YOU! I'M STARING STRAIGHT UP YOUR NOSE!
SO THERE'S A CAMERA ON THIS THING?
NO! I *AM* "THIS THING." I'M THE SMITHSONIAN ARCHIVE INTERFACE FACILITATOR BUILT INTO YOUR DATABASE ACCESS AND RETRIEVAL CONDUITS!
HUH???
THERE ARE TIMES I *REALLY* WISH I COULD SIGH.
I'M YOUR GUIDE. I'M HERE TO DO --

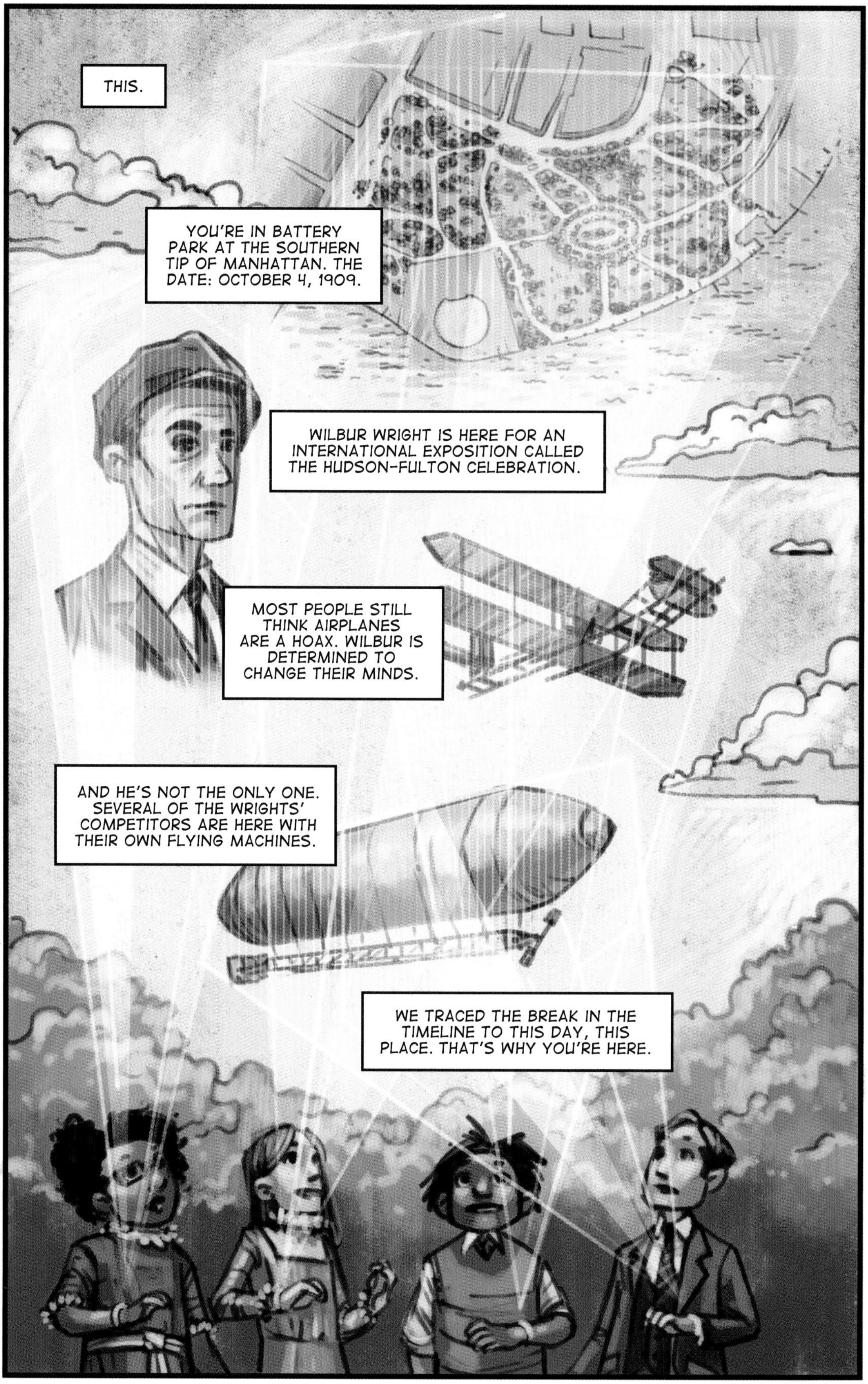
THIS.
YOU'RE IN BATTERY PARK AT THE SOUTHERN TIP OF MANHATTAN. THE DATE: OCTOBER 4, 1909.
WILBUR WRIGHT IS HERE FOR AN INTERNATIONAL EXPOSITION CALLED THE HUDSON-FULTON CELEBRATION.
MOST PEOPLE STILL THINK AIRPLANES ARE A HOAX. WILBUR IS DETERMINED TO CHANGE THEIR MINDS.
AND HE'S NOT THE ONLY ONE. SEVERAL OF THE WRIGHTS' COMPETITORS ARE HERE WITH THEIR OWN FLYING MACHINES.
WE TRACED THE BREAK IN THE TIMELINE TO THIS DAY, THIS PLACE. THAT'S WHY YOU'RE HERE.

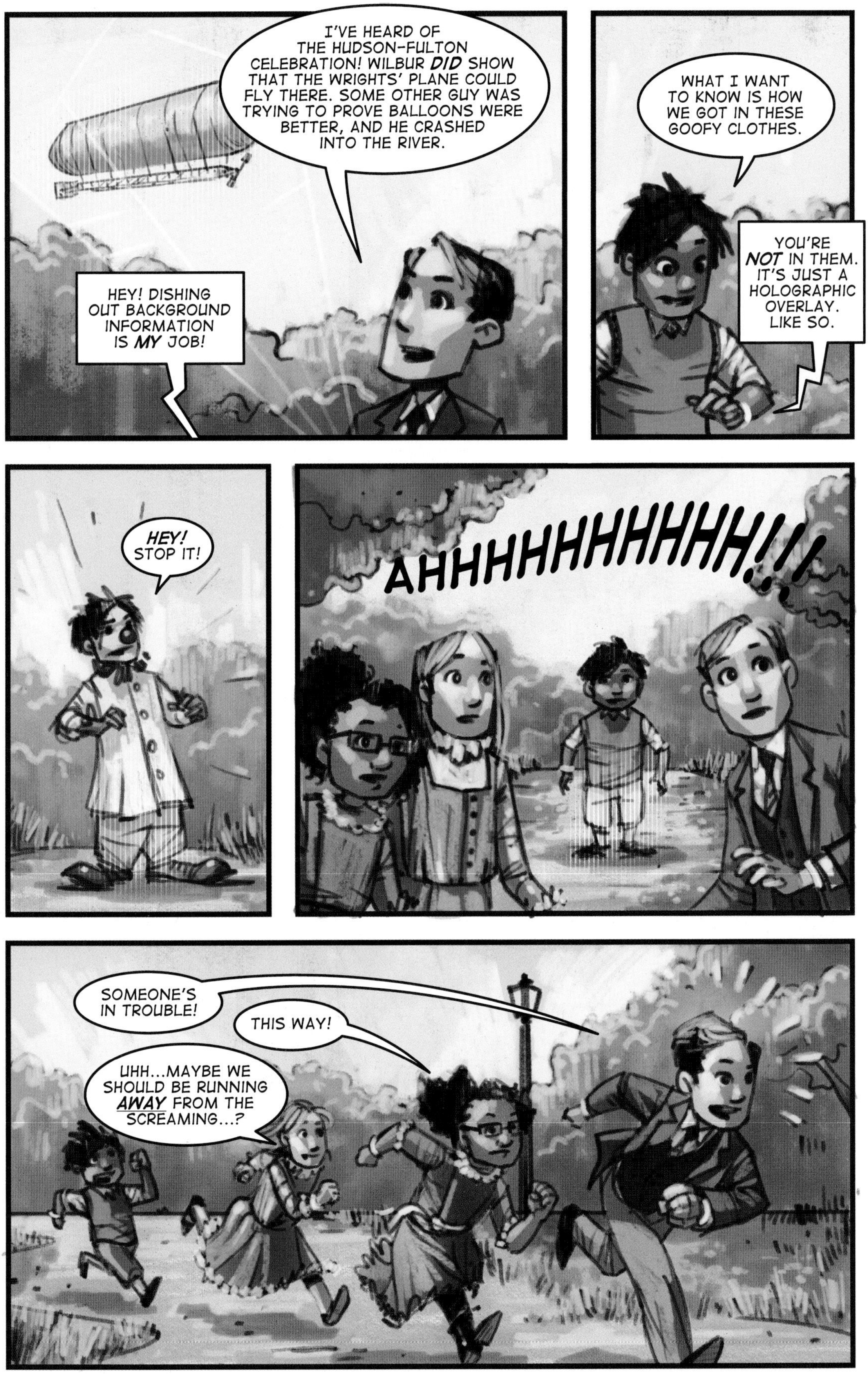
I'VE HEARD OF THE HUDSON-FULTON CELEBRATION! WILBUR DID SHOW THAT THE WRIGHTS' PLANE COULD FLY THERE. SOME OTHER GUY WAS TRYING TO PROVE BALLOONS WERE BETTER, AND HE CRASHED INTO THE RIVER.
HEY! DISHING OUT BACKGROUND INFORMATION IS MY JOB!
WHAT I WANT TO KNOW IS HOW WE GOT IN THESE GOOFY CLOTHES.
YOU'RE NOT IN THEM. IT'S JUST A HOLOGRAPHIC OVERLAY. LIKE SO.
HEY! STOP IT!
AHHHHHHHHHHH!!!
SOMEONE'S IN TROUBLE!
THIS WAY!
UHH...MAYBE WE SHOULD BE RUNNING AWAY FROM THE SCREAMING...?

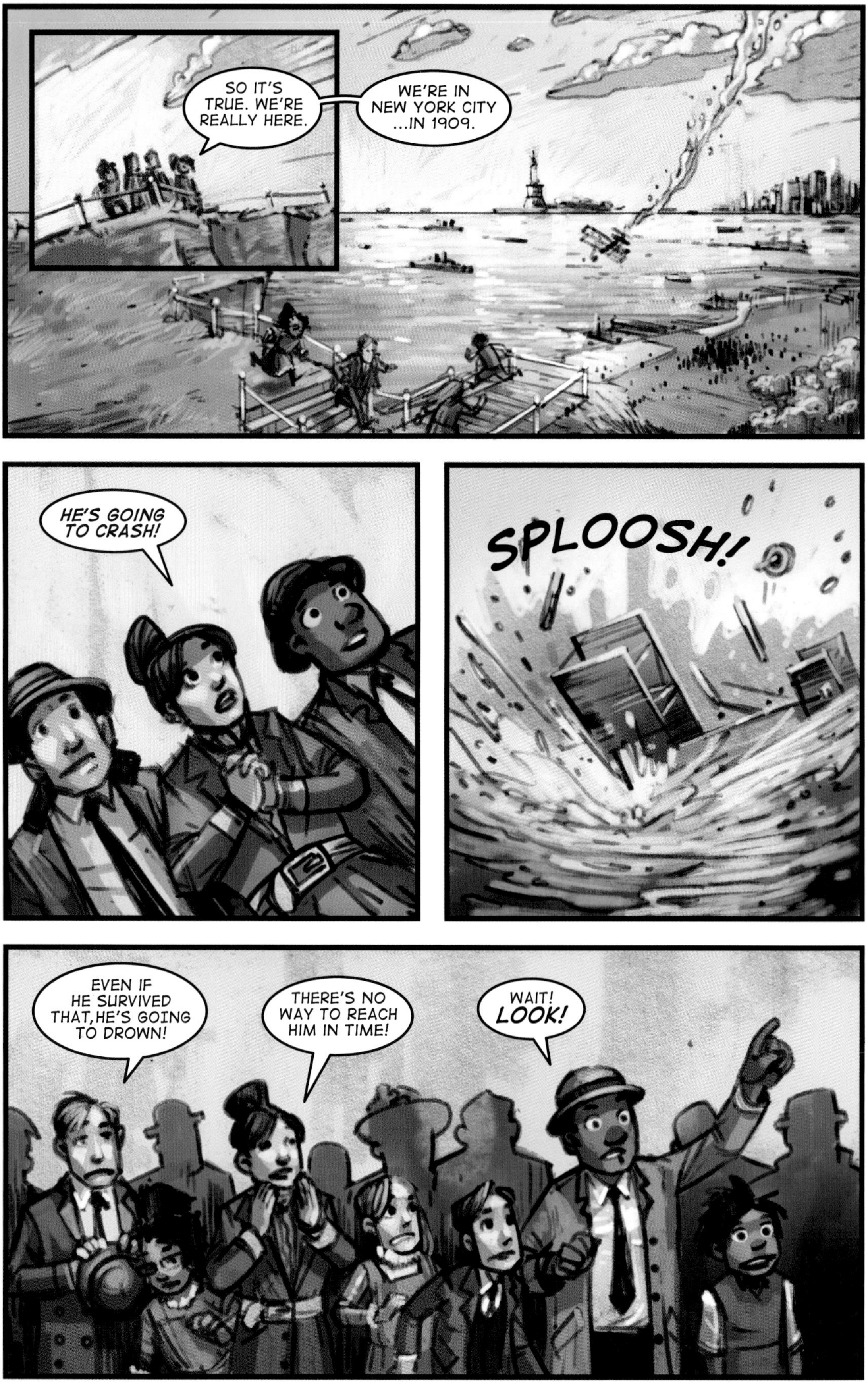
SO IT'S TRUE. WE'RE REALLY HERE.
WE'RE IN NEW YORK CITY ...IN 1909.
HE'S GOING TO CRASH!
SPLOOSH!
EVEN IF HE SURVIVED THAT, HE'S GOING TO DROWN!
THERE'S NO WAY TO REACH HIM IN TIME!
WAIT! LOOK!

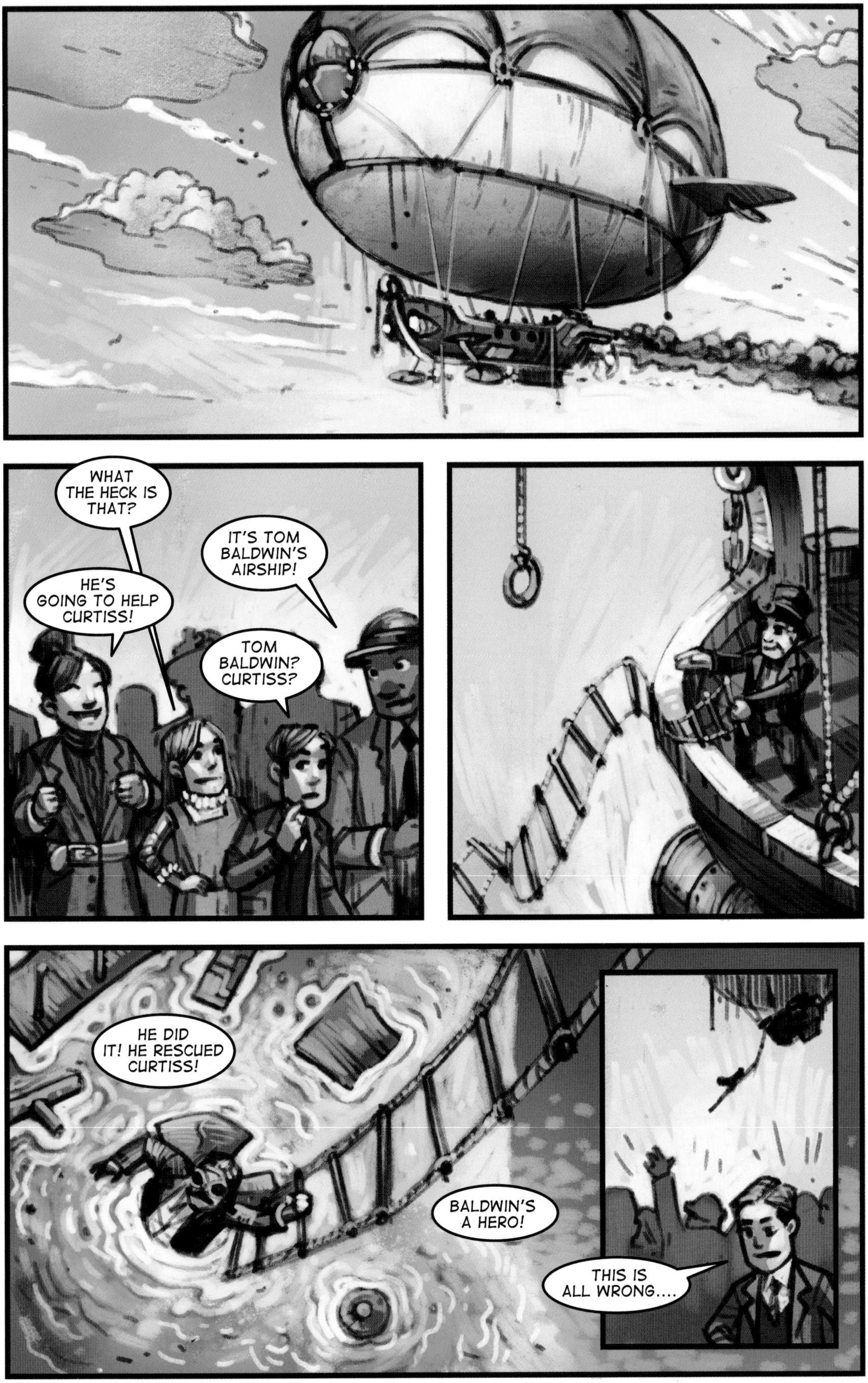
WHAT THE HECK IS THAT?
IT'S TOM BALDWIN'S AIRSHIP!
HE'S GOING TO HELP CURTISS!
TOM BALDWIN? CURTISS?
HE DID IT! HE RESCUED CURTISS!
BALDWIN'S A HERO!
THIS IS ALL WRONG....

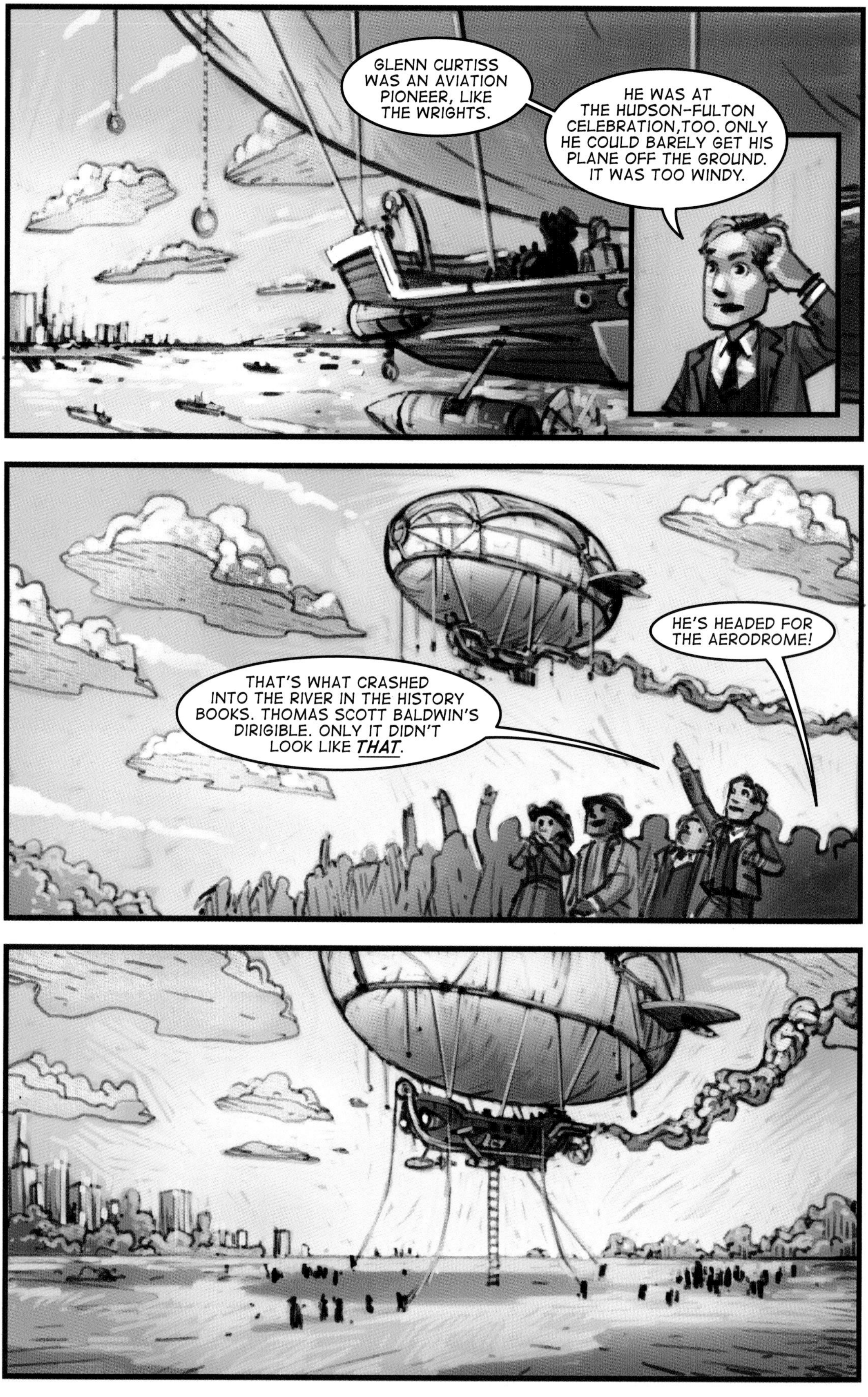
GLENN CURTISS WAS AN AVIATION PIONEER, LIKE THE WRIGHTS.
HE WAS AT THE HUDSON-FULTON CELEBRATION,TOO. ONLY HE COULD BARELY GET HIS PLANE OFF THE GROUND. IT WAS TOO WINDY.
THAT'S WHAT CRASHED INTO THE RIVER IN THE HISTORY BOOKS. THOMAS SCOTT BALDWIN'S DIRIGIBLE. ONLY IT DIDN'T LOOK LIKE THAT.
HE'S HEADED FOR THE AERODROME!

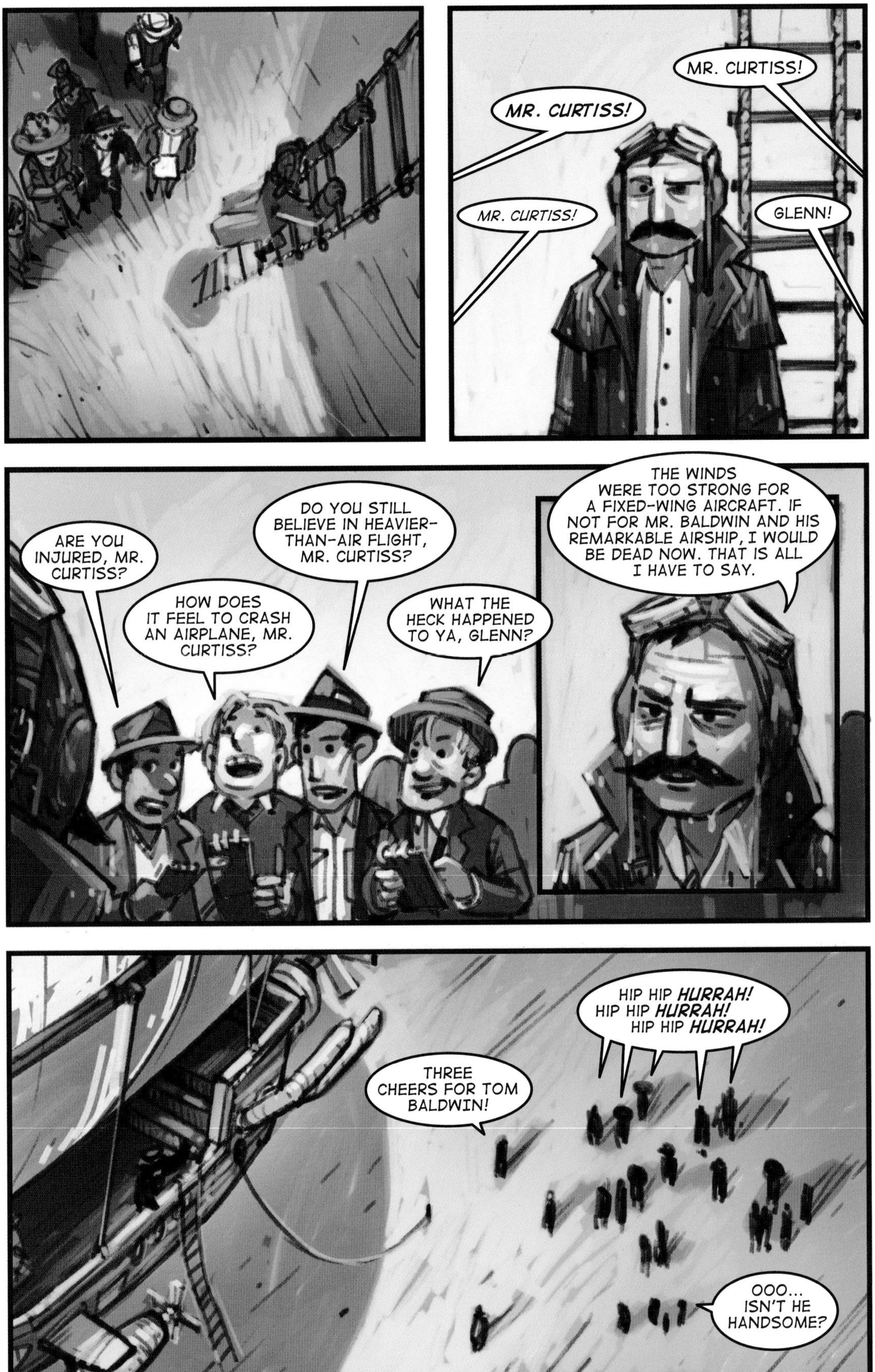
MR. CURTISS!
MR. CURTISS!
MR. CURTISS!
GLENN!
ARE YOU INJURED, MR. CURTISS?
HOW DOES IT FEEL TO CRASH AN AIRPLANE, MR. CURTISS?
DO YOU STILL BELIEVE IN HEAVIER-THAN-AIR FLIGHT, MR. CURTISS?
WHAT THE HECK HAPPENED TO YA, GLENN?
THE WINDS WERE TOO STRONG FOR A FIXED-WING AIRCRAFT. IF NOT FOR MR. BALDWIN AND HIS REMARKABLE AIRSHIP, I WOULD BE DEAD NOW. THAT IS ALL I HAVE TO SAY.
THREE CHEERS FOR TOM BALDWIN!
HIP HIP HURRAH! HIP HIP HURRAH! HIP HIP HURRAH!
OOO... ISN'T HE HANDSOME?

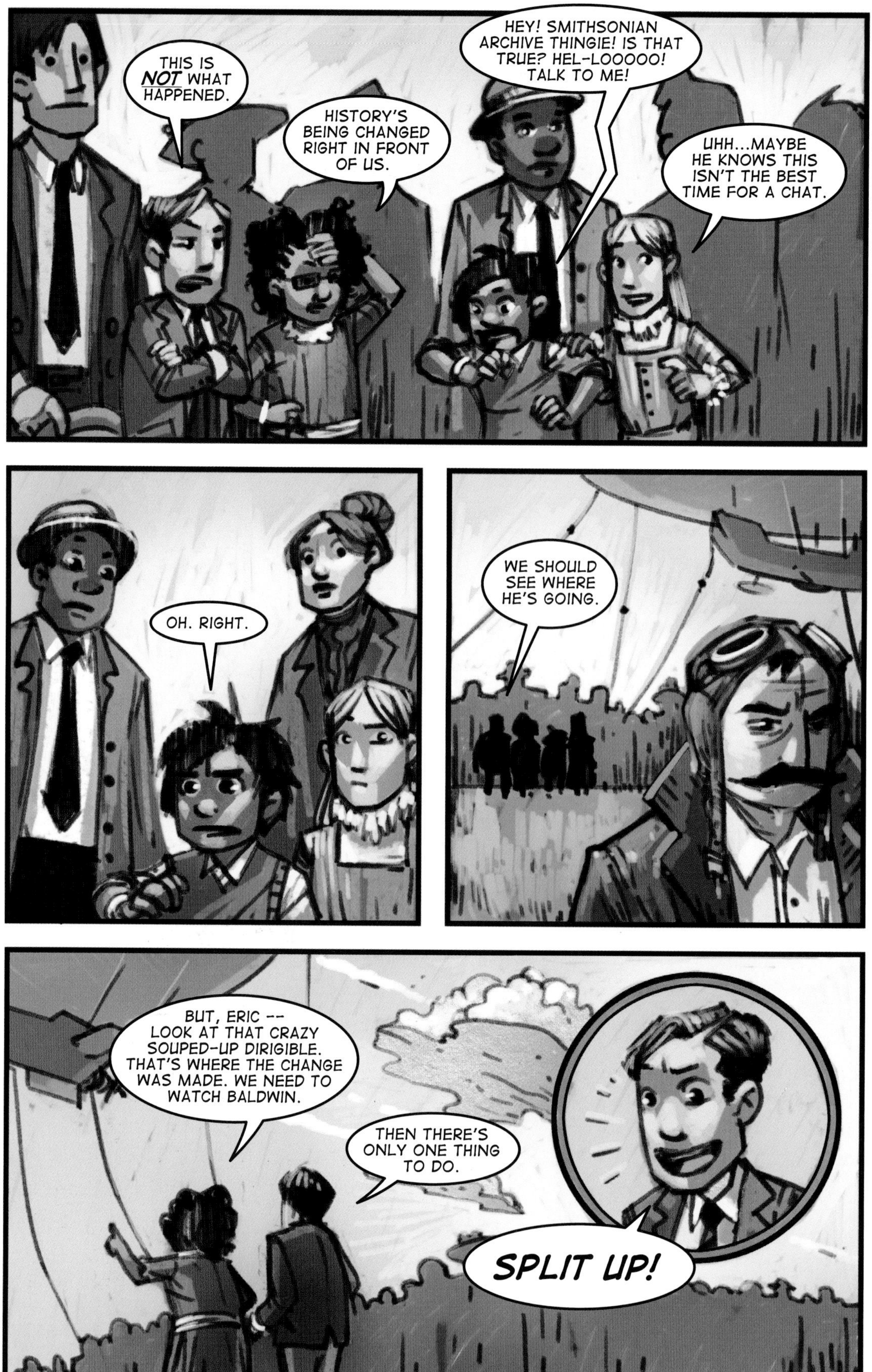
THIS IS NOT WHAT HAPPENED.
HISTORY'S BEING CHANGED RIGHT IN FRONT OF US.
HEY! SMITHSONIAN ARCHIVE THINGIE! IS THAT TRUE? HEL-LOOOOO! TALK TO ME!
UHH...MAYBE HE KNOWS THIS ISN'T THE BEST TIME FOR A CHAT.
OH. RIGHT.
WE SHOULD SEE WHERE HE'S GOING.
BUT, ERIC -- LOOK AT THAT CRAZY SOUPED-UP DIRIGIBLE. THAT'S WHERE THE CHANGE WAS MADE. WE NEED TO WATCH BALDWIN.
THEN THERE'S ONLY ONE THING TO DO.
SPLIT UP!

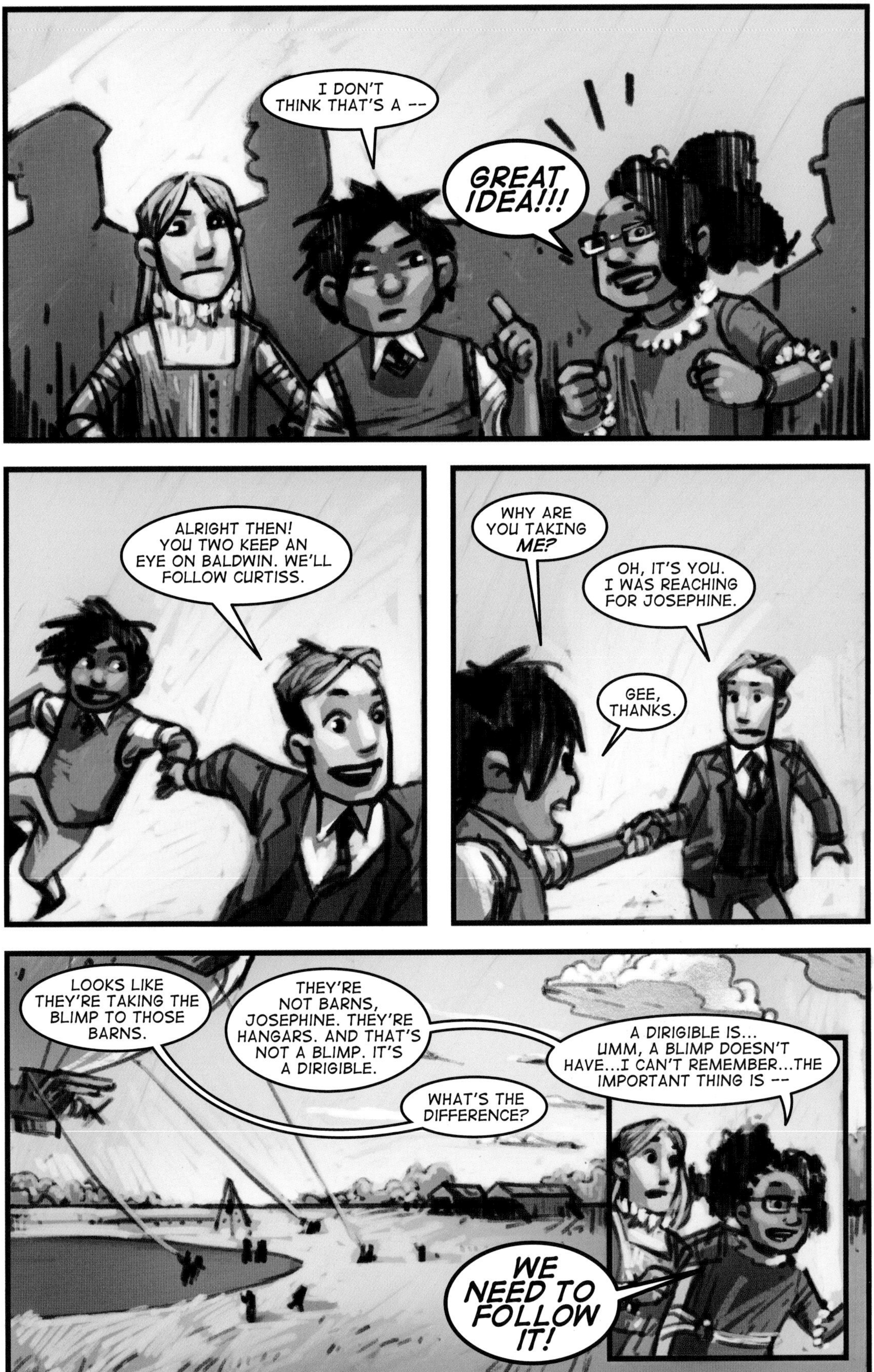
I DON'T THINK THAT'S A --
GREAT IDEA!!!
ALRIGHT THEN! YOU TWO KEEP AN EYE ON BALDWIN. WE'LL FOLLOW CURTISS.
WHY ARE YOU TAKING *ME?*
OH, IT'S YOU. I WAS REACHING FOR JOSEPHINE.
GEE, THANKS.
LOOKS LIKE THEY'RE TAKING THE BLIMP TO THOSE BARNS.
THEY'RE NOT BARNS, JOSEPHINE. THEY'RE HANGARS. AND THAT'S NOT A BLIMP. IT'S A DIRIGIBLE.
WHAT'S THE DIFFERENCE?
A DIRIGIBLE IS... UMM, A BLIMP DOESN'T HAVE...I CAN'T REMEMBER...THE IMPORTANT THING IS --
WE NEED TO FOLLOW IT!

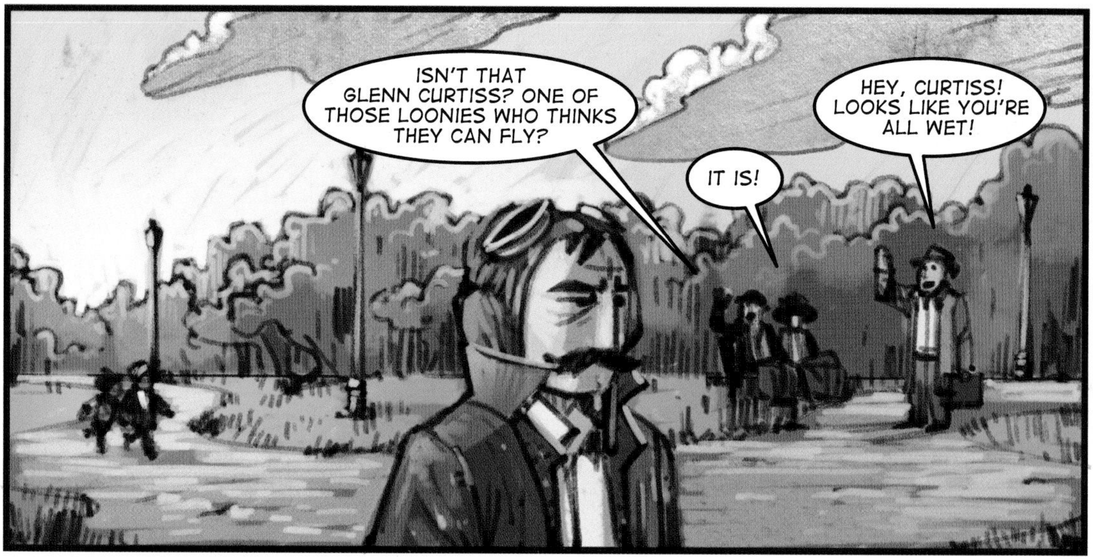
ISN'T THAT GLENN CURTISS? ONE OF THOSE LOONIES WHO THINKS THEY CAN FLY?
IT IS!
HEY, CURTISS! LOOKS LIKE YOU'RE ALL WET!

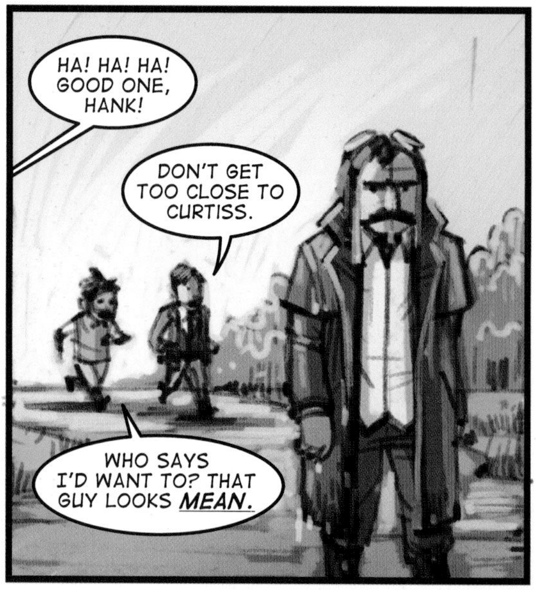
HA! HA! HA! GOOD ONE, HANK!
DON'T GET TOO CLOSE TO CURTISS.
WHO SAYS I'D WANT TO? THAT GUY LOOKS MEAN.

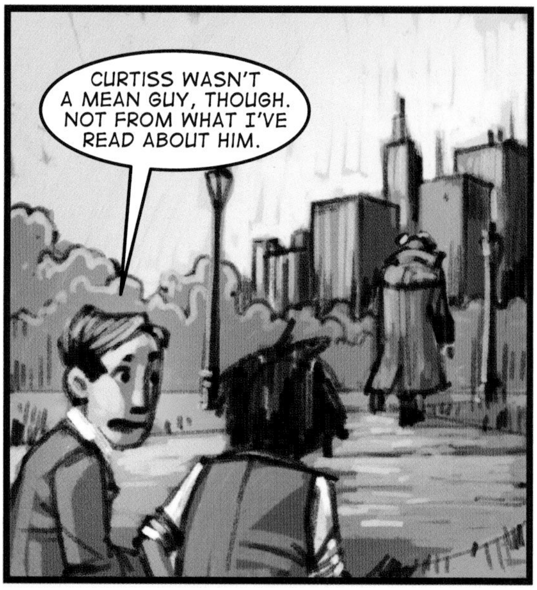
CURTISS WASN'T A MEAN GUY, THOUGH. NOT FROM WHAT I'VE READ ABOUT HIM.

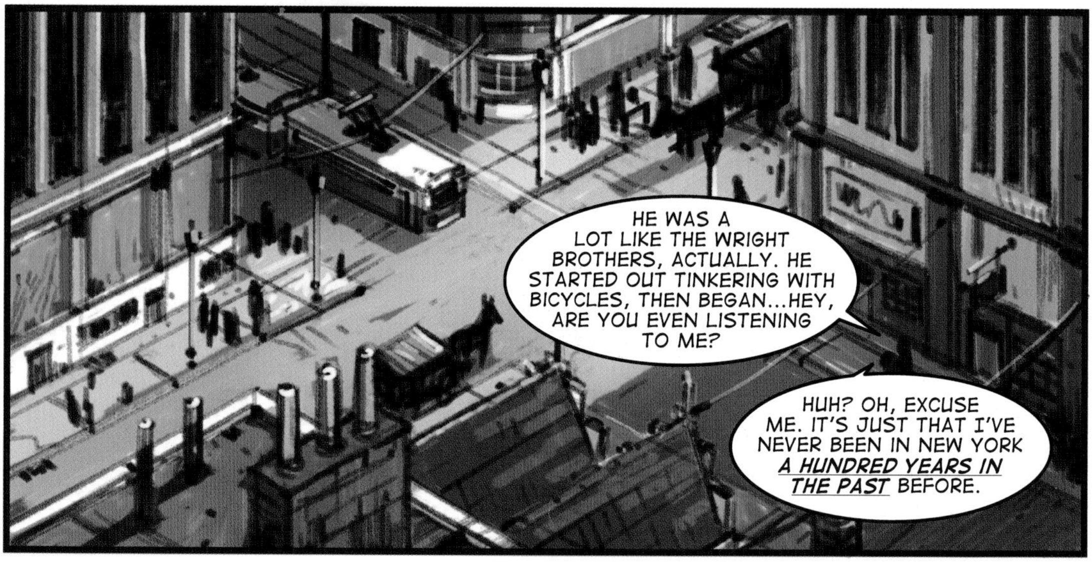
HE WAS A LOT LIKE THE WRIGHT BROTHERS, ACTUALLY. HE STARTED OUT TINKERING WITH BICYCLES, THEN BEGAN...HEY, ARE YOU EVEN LISTENING TO ME?
HUH? OH, EXCUSE ME. IT'S JUST THAT I'VE NEVER BEEN IN NEW YORK A HUNDRED YEARS IN THE PAST BEFORE.

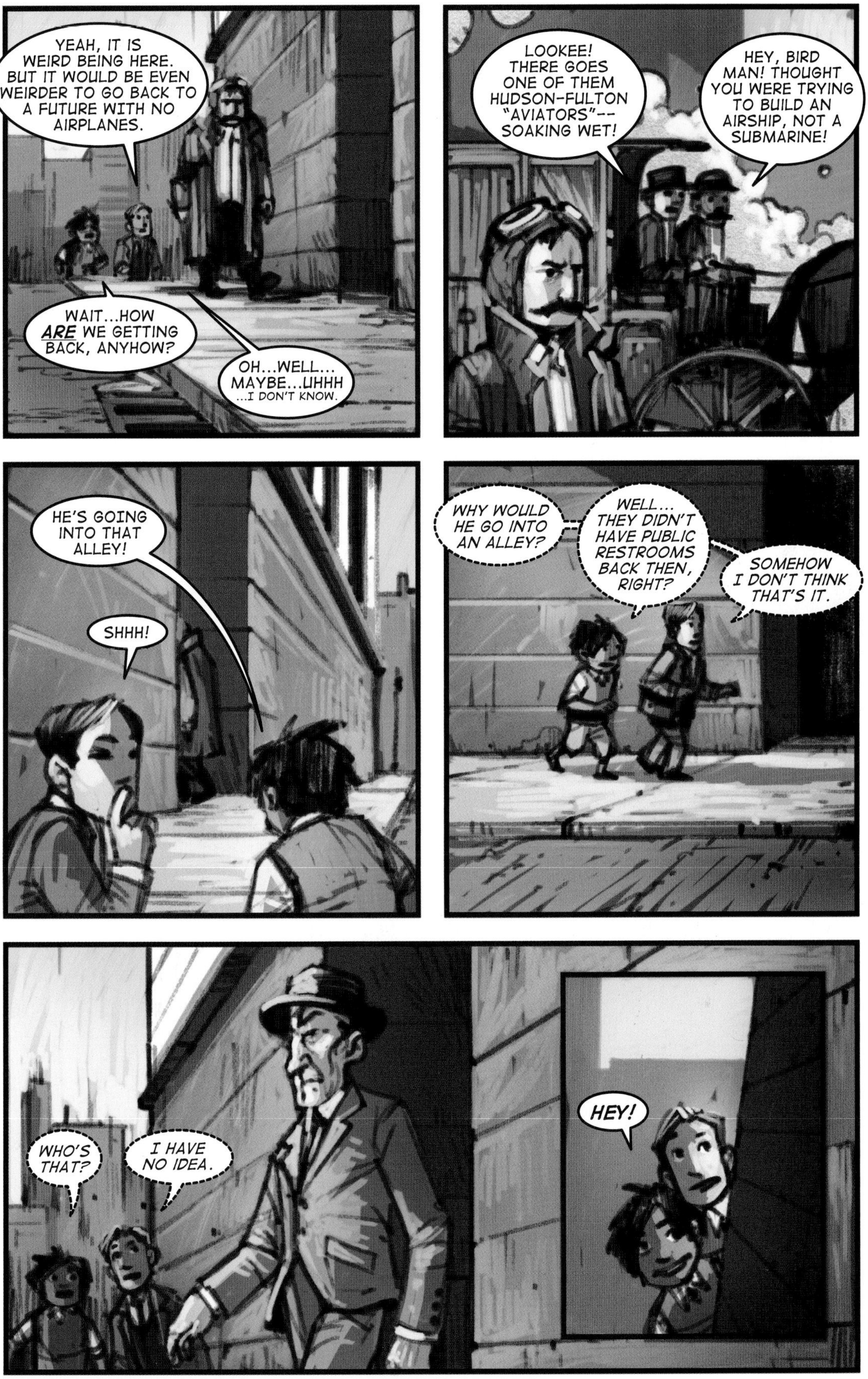
YEAH, IT IS WEIRD BEING HERE. BUT IT WOULD BE EVEN WEIRDER TO GO BACK TO A FUTURE WITH NO AIRPLANES.
WAIT...HOW ARE WE GETTING BACK, ANYHOW?
OH...WELL... MAYBE...UHHH ...I DON'T KNOW.
LOOKEE! THERE GOES ONE OF THEM HUDSON-FULTON "AVIATORS"-- SOAKING WET!
HEY, BIRD MAN! THOUGHT YOU WERE TRYING TO BUILD AN AIRSHIP, NOT A SUBMARINE!
HE'S GOING INTO THAT ALLEY!
SHHH!
WHY WOULD HE GO INTO AN ALLEY?
WELL... THEY DIDN'T HAVE PUBLIC RESTROOMS BACK THEN, RIGHT?
SOMEHOW I DON'T THINK THAT'S IT.
WHO'S THAT?
I HAVE NO IDEA.
HEY!

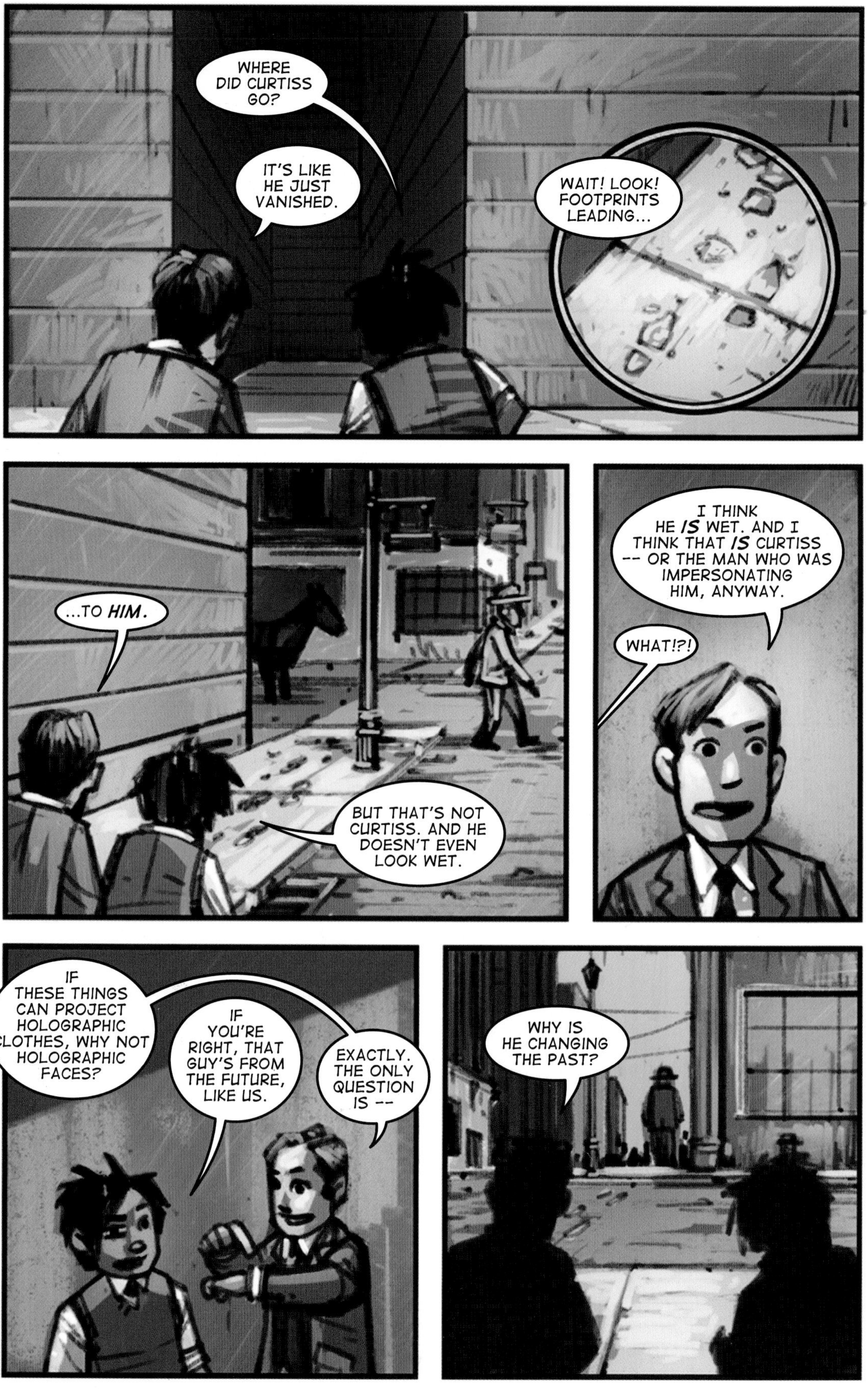
WHERE DID CURTISS GO?
IT'S LIKE HE JUST VANISHED.
WAIT! LOOK! FOOTPRINTS LEADING...
...TO *HIM*.
BUT THAT'S NOT CURTISS. AND HE DOESN'T EVEN LOOK WET.
I THINK HE *IS* WET. AND I THINK THAT *IS* CURTISS -- OR THE MAN WHO WAS IMPERSONATING HIM, ANYWAY.
WHAT!?!
IF THESE THINGS CAN PROJECT HOLOGRAPHIC CLOTHES, WHY NOT HOLOGRAPHIC FACES?
IF YOU'RE RIGHT, THAT GUY'S FROM THE FUTURE, LIKE US.
EXACTLY. THE ONLY QUESTION IS --
WHY IS HE CHANGING THE PAST?

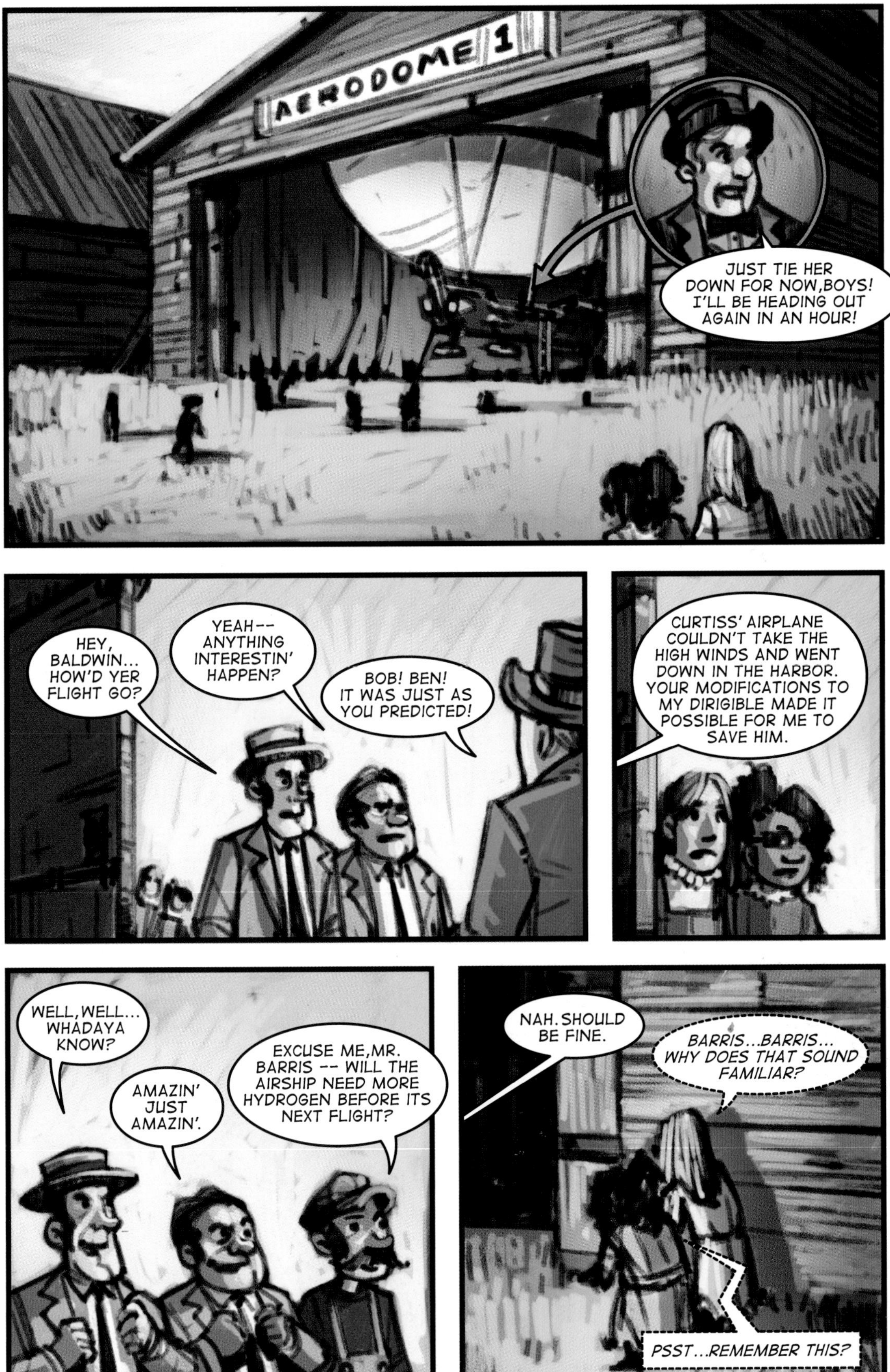
AERODOME 1
JUST TIE HER DOWN FOR NOW, BOYS! I'LL BE HEADING OUT AGAIN IN AN HOUR!
HEY, BALDWIN... HOW'D YER FLIGHT GO?
YEAH-- ANYTHING INTERESTIN' HAPPEN?
BOB! BEN! IT WAS JUST AS YOU PREDICTED!
CURTISS' AIRPLANE COULDN'T TAKE THE HIGH WINDS AND WENT DOWN IN THE HARBOR. YOUR MODIFICATIONS TO MY DIRIGIBLE MADE IT POSSIBLE FOR ME TO SAVE HIM.
WELL, WELL... WHADAYA KNOW?
AMAZIN' JUST AMAZIN'.
EXCUSE ME, MR. BARRIS -- WILL THE AIRSHIP NEED MORE HYDROGEN BEFORE ITS NEXT FLIGHT?
NAH. SHOULD BE FINE.
BARRIS...BARRIS... WHY DOES THAT SOUND FAMILIAR?
PSST...REMEMBER THIS?

HEY -- THAT WAS ON ALL THOSE BLIMPS IN THE MUSEUM.
YOU'RE RIGHT!
BARRIS BA AIR
GLAD YOU'LL BE IN THE AIR AGAIN WHEN WRIGHT TRIES TA FLY LATER. HE MIGHT BE AS UNLUCKY AS CURTISS.
SO LONG FOR NOW, BALDWIN! ME AND MY BROTHER GOTS MORE INVESTORS TA MEET WITH. THEY'RE GONNA BE MIGHTY INTERESTED AFTER WHAT JUST HAPPENED!
IT'S THEM. THEY'RE THE ONES CHANGING HISTORY. THEY'RE GIVING THEIR ANCESTORS CONTROL OF AVIATION.
MAYBE NOT THEIR ANCESTORS.
WE'RE IN THE MONEY...
WE'RE IN THE MONEY...
WE'VE GOT A LOT OF WHAT IT TAKES TO GET ALONG....
HEY, COMPUTER DUDE -- HOW OLD IS THE SONG "WE'RE IN THE MONEY"?
ITS ACTUAL TITLE IS "THE GOLD DIGGERS' SONG." IT WAS WRITTEN FOR THE FILM GOLD DIGGERS OF 1933 -- 24 YEARS FROM NOW.
AND DON'T CALL ME "COMPUTER DUDE."
I KNEW IT. THAT SONG'S IN, LIKE, A MILLION BUGS BUNNY CARTOONS.
NEVER MIND THAT -- COME ON! OBVIOUSLY THOSE GUYS ARE FROM THE FUTURE, TOO...WHICH MEANS THEY'RE THE KEY TO EVERYTHING!

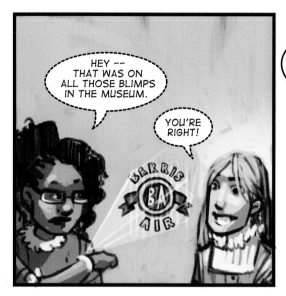

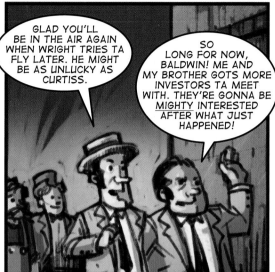

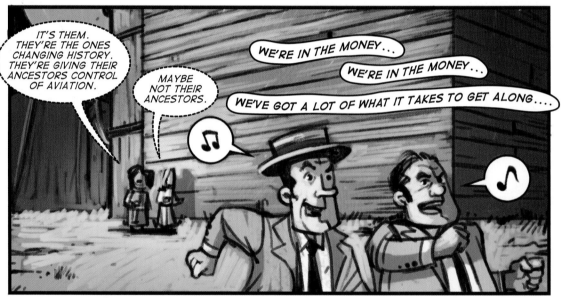

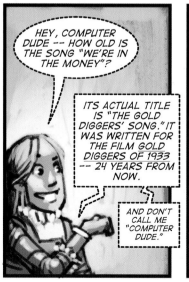

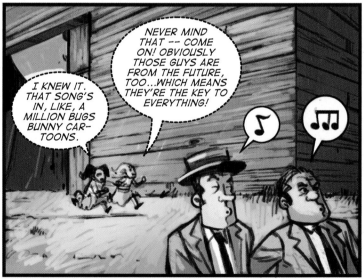

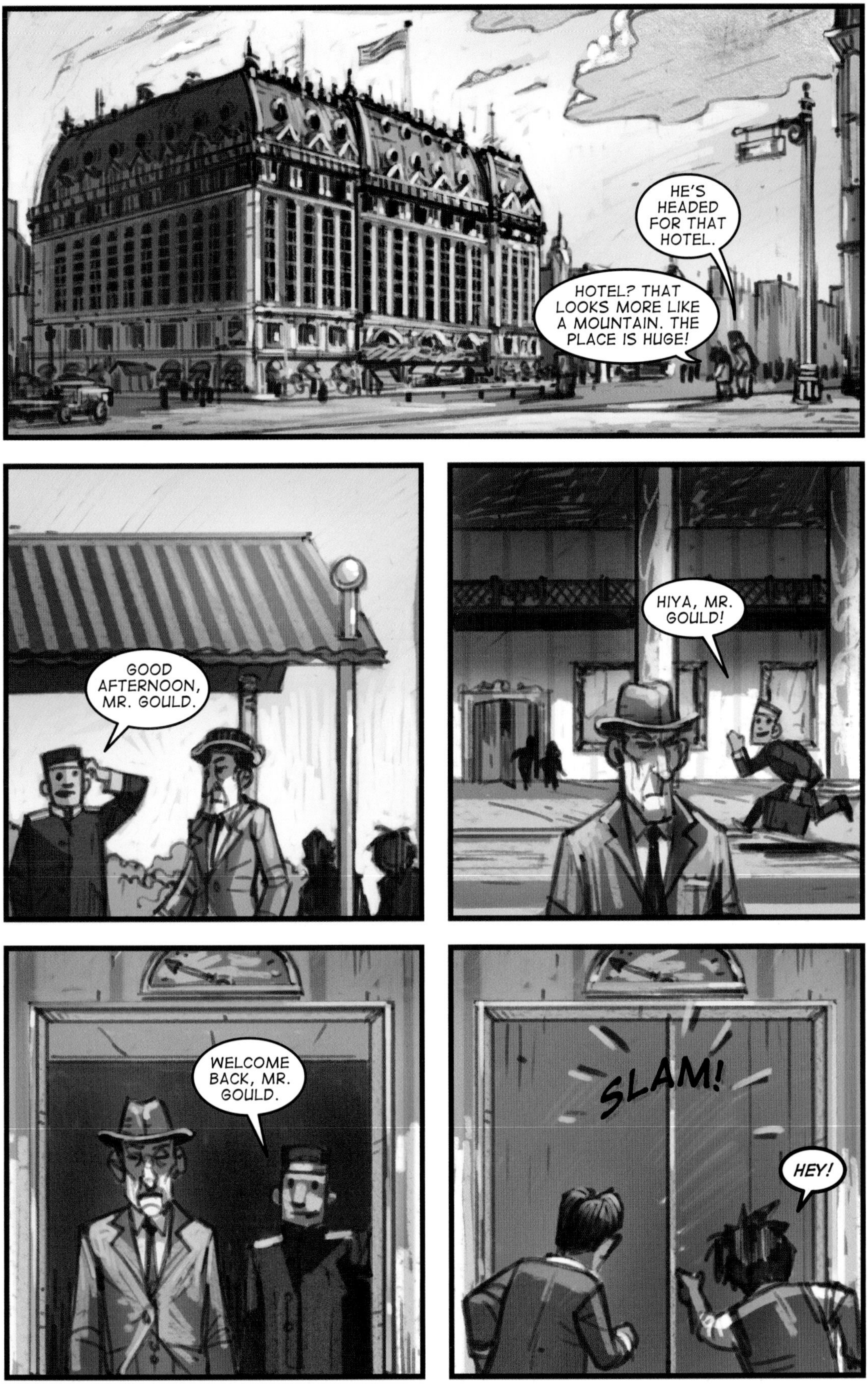
HE'S HEADED FOR THAT HOTEL.
HOTEL? THAT LOOKS MORE LIKE A MOUNTAIN. THE PLACE IS HUGE!
GOOD AFTERNOON, MR. GOULD.
HIYA, MR. GOULD!
WELCOME BACK, MR. GOULD.
SLAM!
HEY!

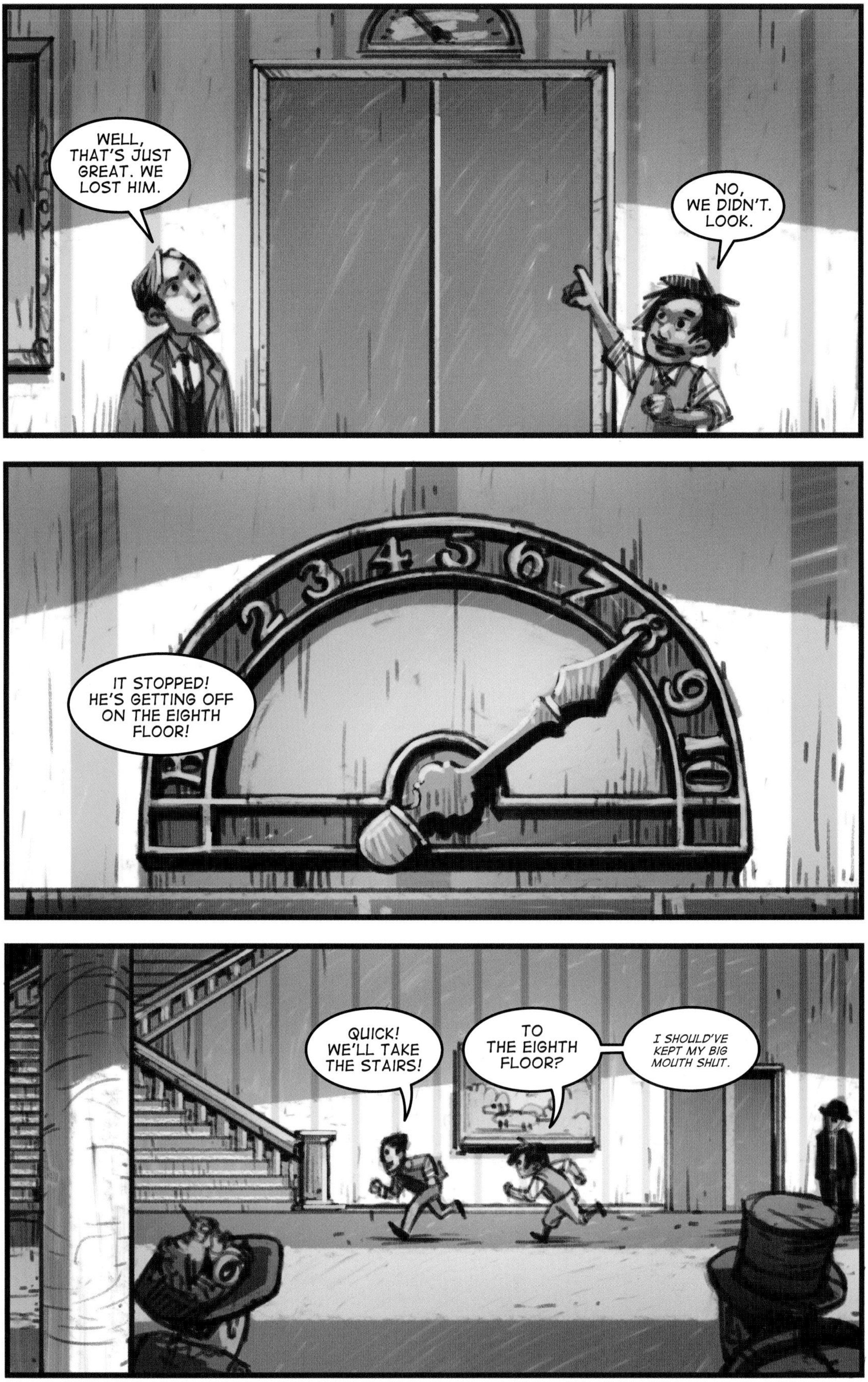
WELL, THAT'S JUST GREAT. WE LOST HIM.
NO, WE DIDN'T. LOOK.
IT STOPPED! HE'S GETTING OFF ON THE EIGHTH FLOOR!
QUICK! WE'LL TAKE THE STAIRS!
TO THE EIGHTH FLOOR?
I SHOULD'VE KEPT MY BIG MOUTH SHUT.

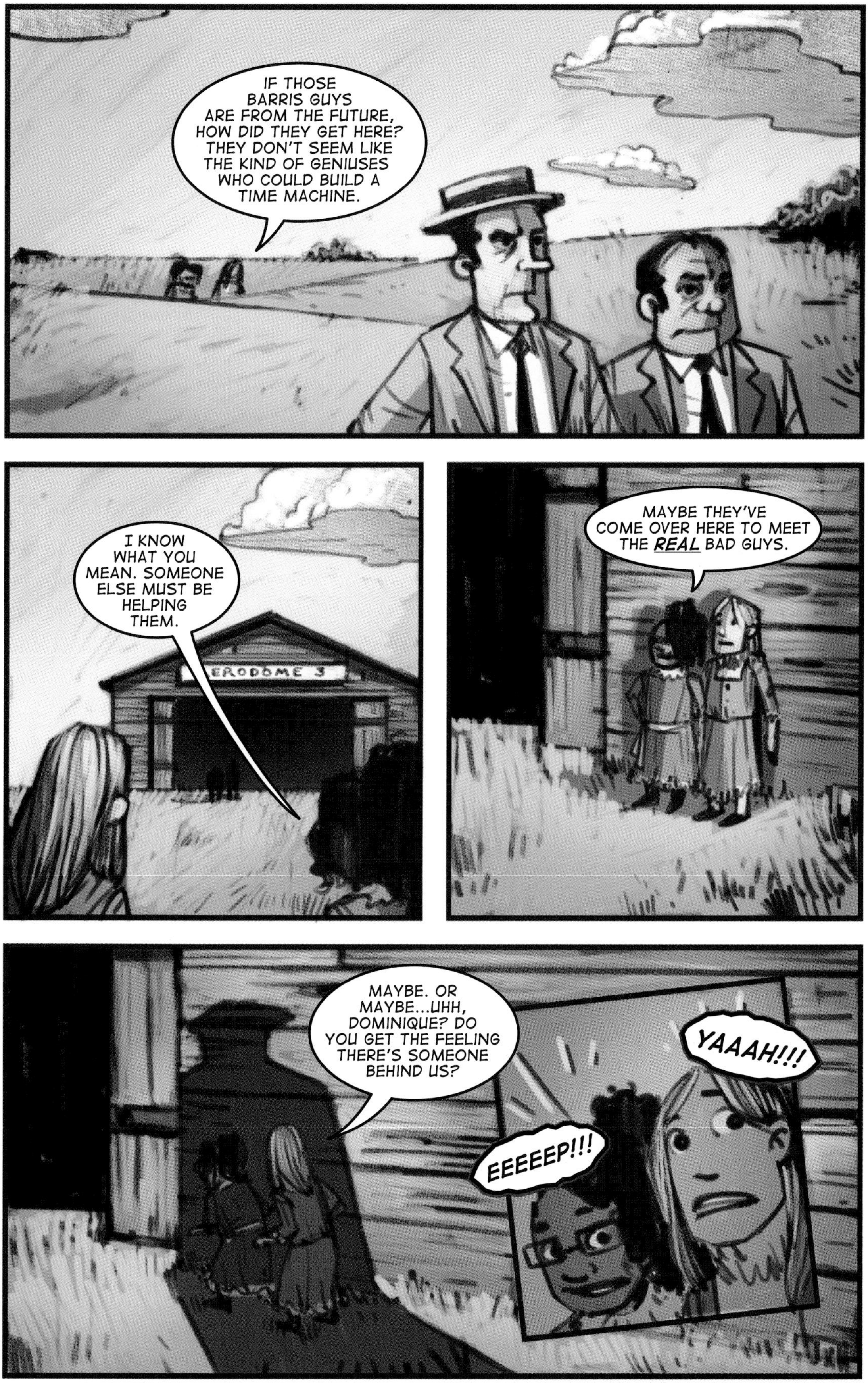
IF THOSE BARRIS GUYS ARE FROM THE FUTURE, HOW DID THEY GET HERE? THEY DON'T SEEM LIKE THE KIND OF GENIUSES WHO COULD BUILD A TIME MACHINE.
I KNOW WHAT YOU MEAN. SOMEONE ELSE MUST BE HELPING THEM.
ERODOME 3
MAYBE THEY'VE COME OVER HERE TO MEET THE REAL BAD GUYS.
MAYBE. OR MAYBE...UHH, DOMINIQUE? DO YOU GET THE FEELING THERE'S SOMEONE BEHIND US?
YAAAH!!!
EEEEEP!!!

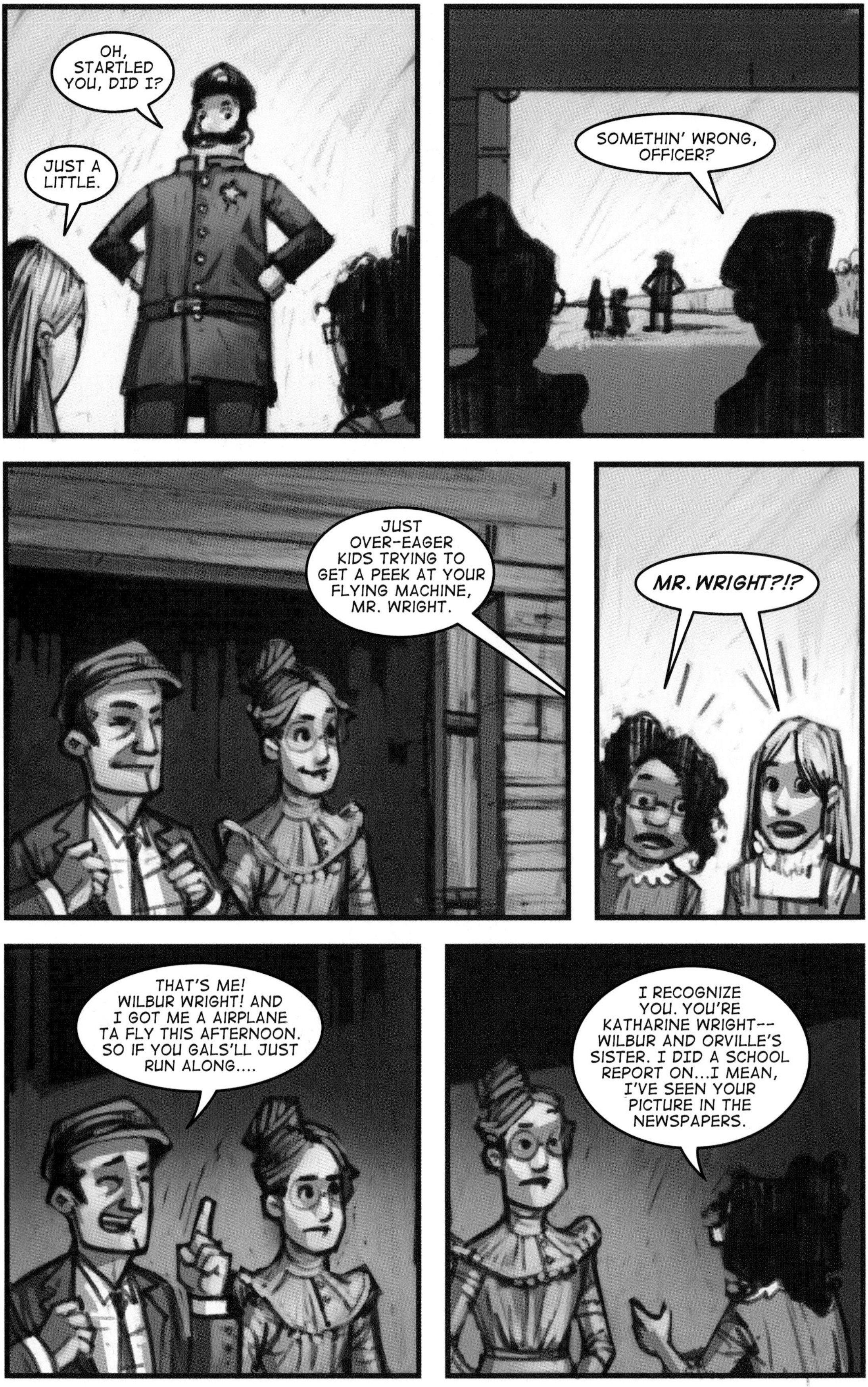
OH, STARTLED YOU, DID I?
JUST A LITTLE.
SOMETHIN' WRONG, OFFICER?
JUST OVER-EAGER KIDS TRYING TO GET A PEEK AT YOUR FLYING MACHINE, MR. WRIGHT.
MR. WRIGHT?!?
THAT'S ME! WILBUR WRIGHT! AND I GOT ME A AIRPLANE TA FLY THIS AFTERNOON. SO IF YOU GALS'LL JUST RUN ALONG....
I RECOGNIZE YOU. YOU'RE KATHARINE WRIGHT--WILBUR AND ORVILLE'S SISTER. I DID A SCHOOL REPORT ON...I MEAN, I'VE SEEN YOUR PICTURE IN THE NEWSPAPERS.

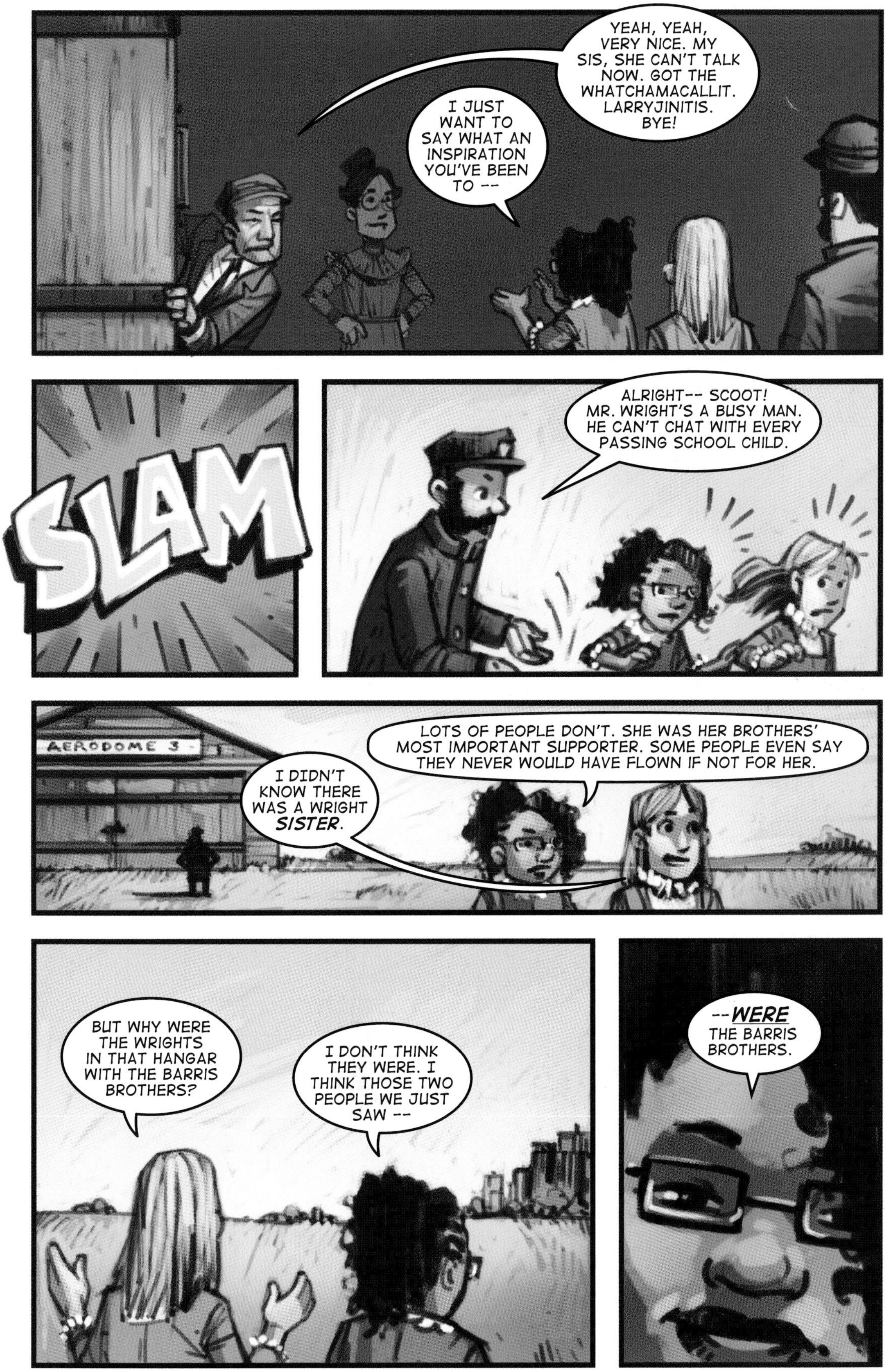
I JUST WANT TO SAY WHAT AN INSPIRATION YOU'VE BEEN TO --
YEAH, YEAH, VERY NICE. MY SIS, SHE CAN'T TALK NOW. GOT THE WHATCHAMACALLIT. LARRYJINITIS. BYE!
SLAM
ALRIGHT-- SCOOT! MR. WRIGHT'S A BUSY MAN. HE CAN'T CHAT WITH EVERY PASSING SCHOOL CHILD.
AERODOME 3
I DIDN'T KNOW THERE WAS A WRIGHT *SISTER*.
LOTS OF PEOPLE DON'T. SHE WAS HER BROTHERS' MOST IMPORTANT SUPPORTER. SOME PEOPLE EVEN SAY THEY NEVER WOULD HAVE FLOWN IF NOT FOR HER.
BUT WHY WERE THE WRIGHTS IN THAT HANGAR WITH THE BARRIS BROTHERS?
I DON'T THINK THEY WERE. I THINK THOSE TWO PEOPLE WE JUST SAW --
--***WERE*** THE BARRIS BROTHERS.

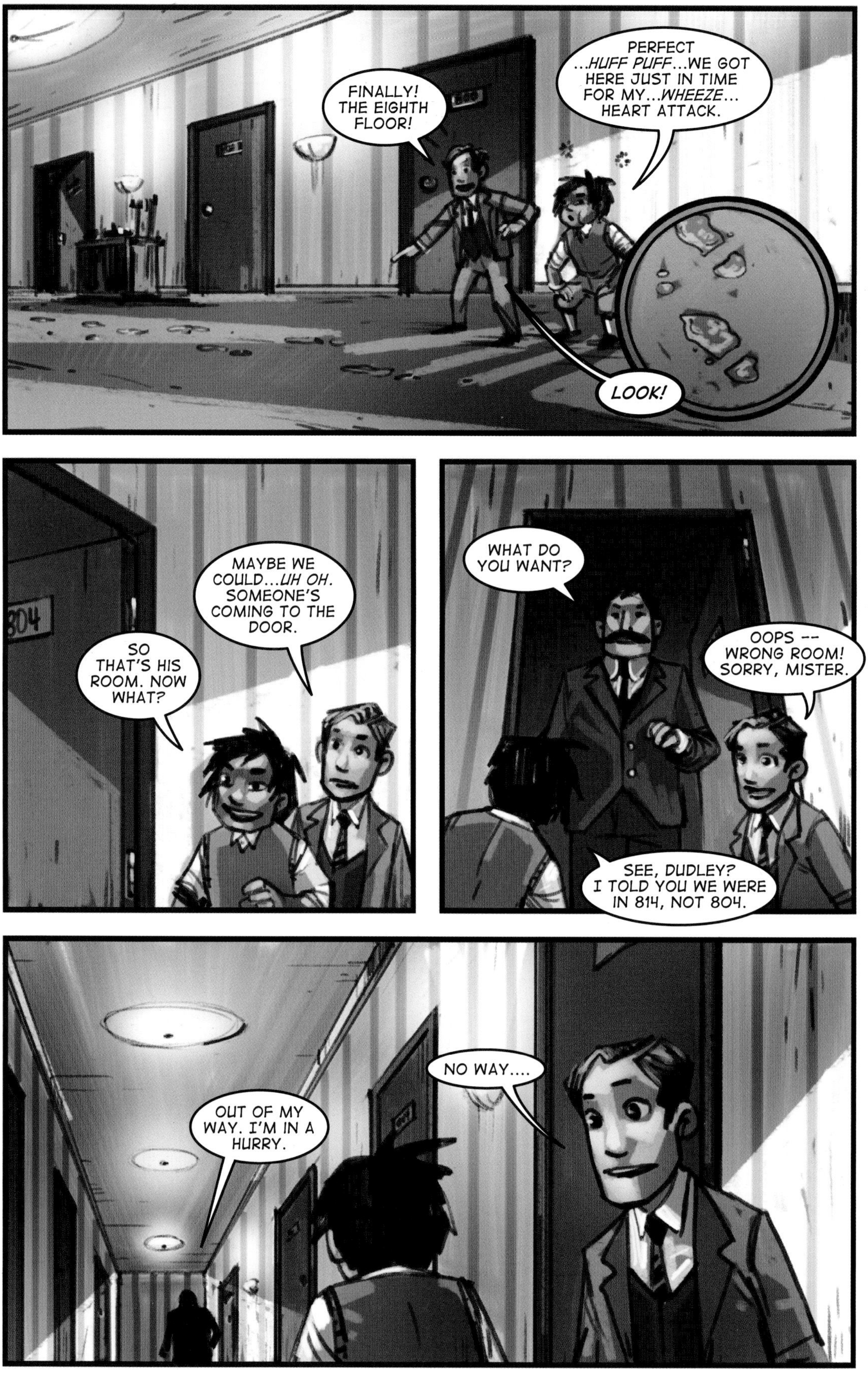
FINALLY! THE EIGHTH FLOOR!
PERFECT ...*HUFF PUFF*...WE GOT HERE JUST IN TIME FOR MY...*WHEEZE*... HEART ATTACK.
LOOK!
804
SO THAT'S HIS ROOM. NOW WHAT?
MAYBE WE COULD...*UH OH*. SOMEONE'S COMING TO THE DOOR.
WHAT DO YOU WANT?
OOPS -- WRONG ROOM! SORRY, MISTER.
SEE, DUDLEY? I TOLD YOU WE WERE IN 814, NOT 804.
OUT OF MY WAY. I'M IN A HURRY.
NO WAY....

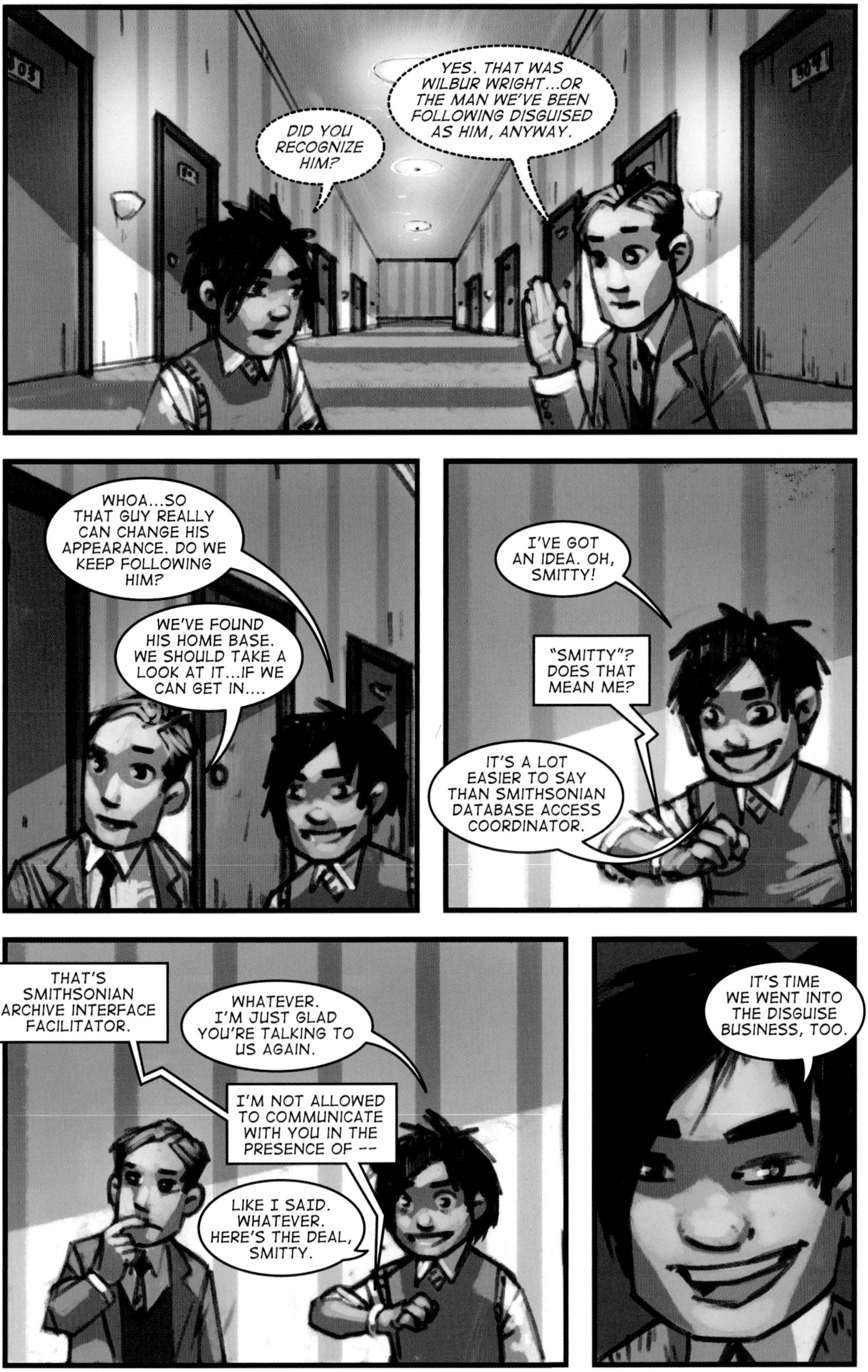
DID YOU RECOGNIZE HIM?
YES. THAT WAS WILBUR WRIGHT...OR THE MAN WE'VE BEEN FOLLOWING DISGUISED AS HIM, ANYWAY.
WHOA...SO THAT GUY REALLY CAN CHANGE HIS APPEARANCE. DO WE KEEP FOLLOWING HIM?
WE'VE FOUND HIS HOME BASE. WE SHOULD TAKE A LOOK AT IT...IF WE CAN GET IN....
I'VE GOT AN IDEA. OH, SMITTY!
"SMITTY"? DOES THAT MEAN ME?
IT'S A LOT EASIER TO SAY THAN SMITHSONIAN DATABASE ACCESS COORDINATOR.
THAT'S SMITHSONIAN ARCHIVE INTERFACE FACILITATOR.
WHATEVER. I'M JUST GLAD YOU'RE TALKING TO US AGAIN.
I'M NOT ALLOWED TO COMMUNICATE WITH YOU IN THE PRESENCE OF --
LIKE I SAID. WHATEVER. HERE'S THE DEAL, SMITTY.
IT'S TIME WE WENT INTO THE DISGUISE BUSINESS, TOO.

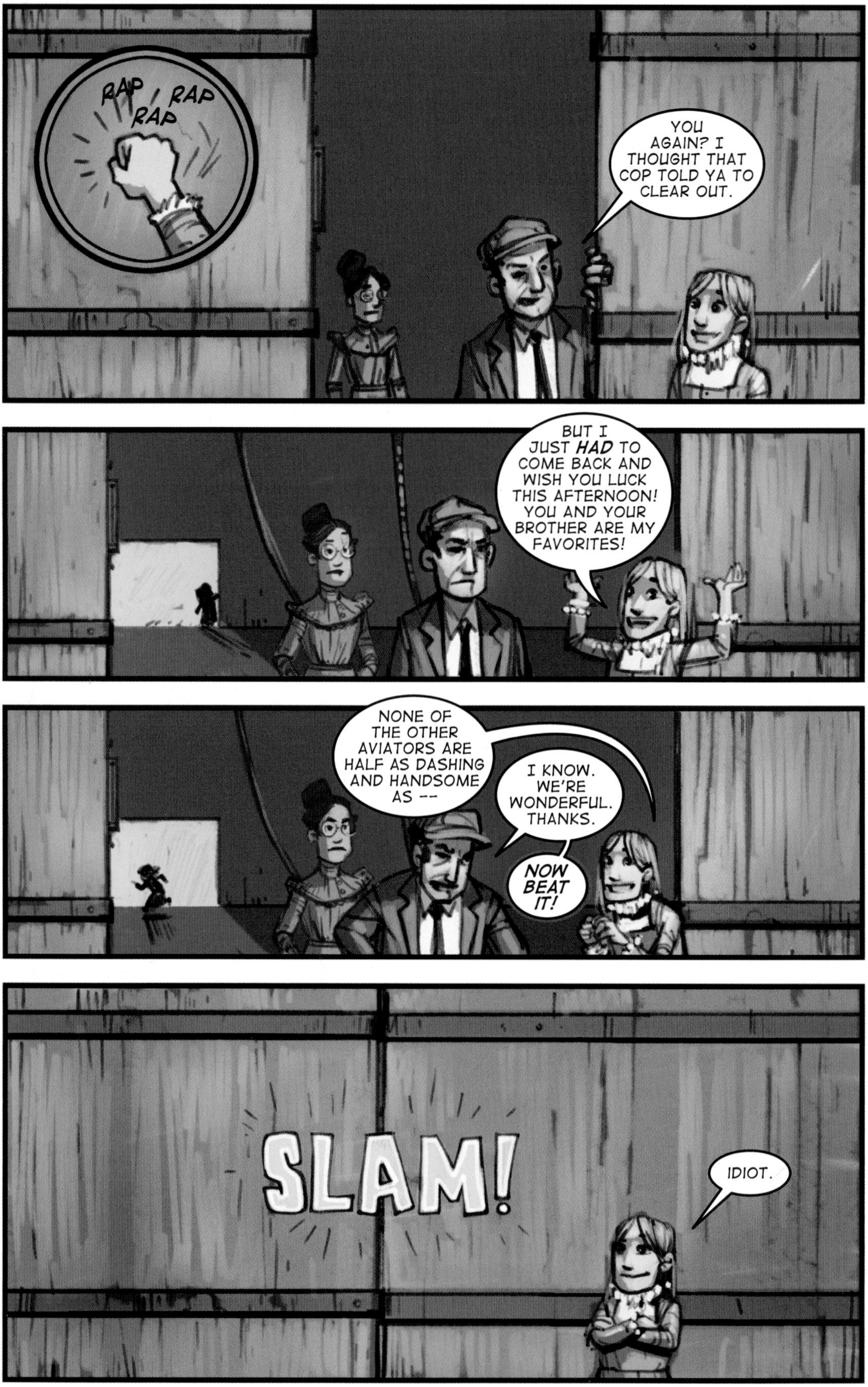
RAP RAP RAP
YOU AGAIN? I THOUGHT THAT COP TOLD YA TO CLEAR OUT.
BUT I JUST **HAD** TO COME BACK AND WISH YOU LUCK THIS AFTERNOON! YOU AND YOUR BROTHER ARE MY FAVORITES!
NONE OF THE OTHER AVIATORS ARE HALF AS DASHING AND HANDSOME AS --
I KNOW. WE'RE WONDERFUL. THANKS.
NOW BEAT IT!
SLAM!
IDIOT.

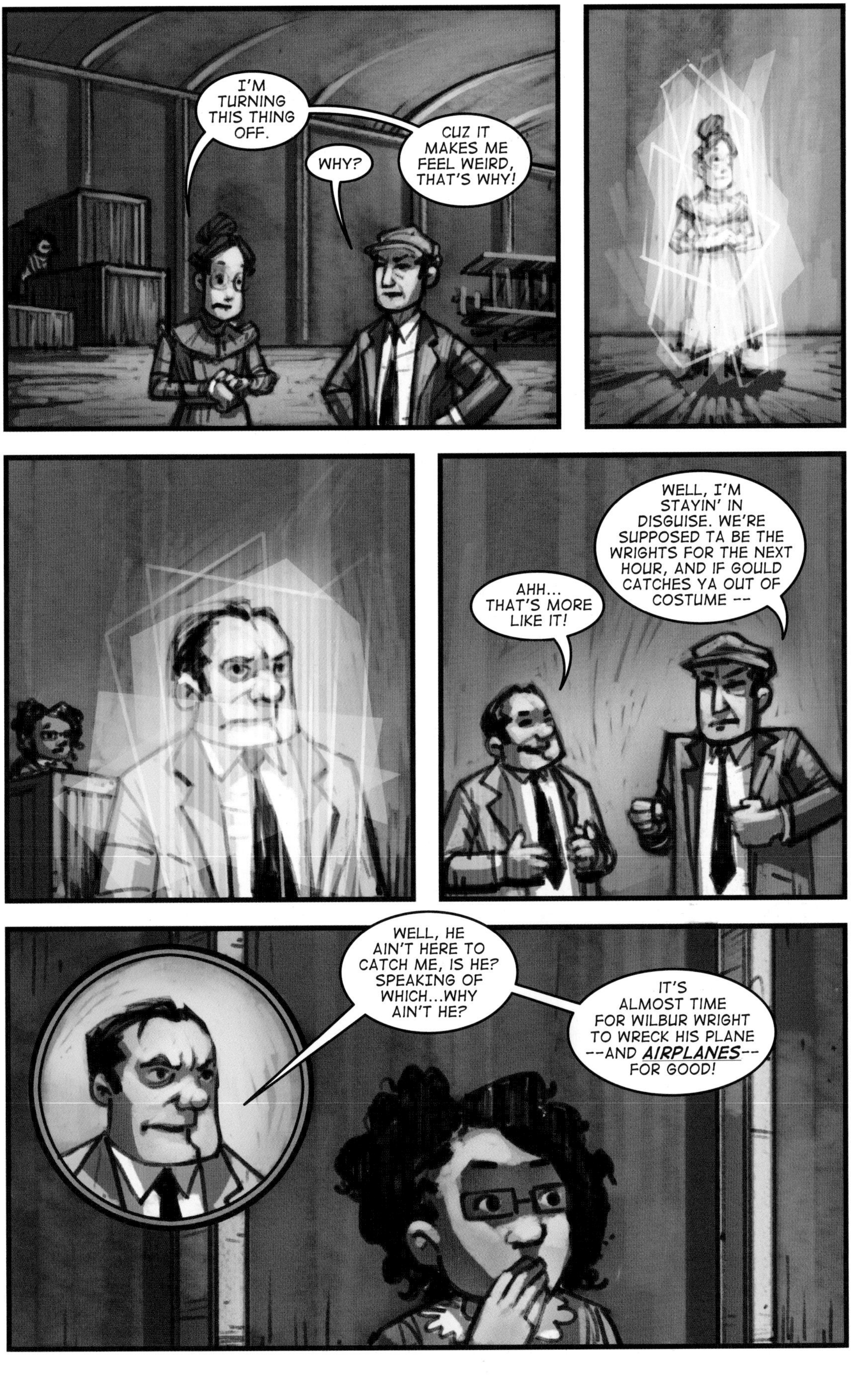
I'M TURNING THIS THING OFF.
WHY?
CUZ IT MAKES ME FEEL WEIRD, THAT'S WHY!
AHH... THAT'S MORE LIKE IT!
WELL, I'M STAYIN' IN DISGUISE. WE'RE SUPPOSED TA BE THE WRIGHTS FOR THE NEXT HOUR, AND IF GOULD CATCHES YA OUT OF COSTUME --
WELL, HE AIN'T HERE TO CATCH ME, IS HE? SPEAKING OF WHICH...WHY AIN'T HE?
IT'S ALMOST TIME FOR WILBUR WRIGHT TO WRECK HIS PLANE --AND AIRPLANES-- FOR GOOD!

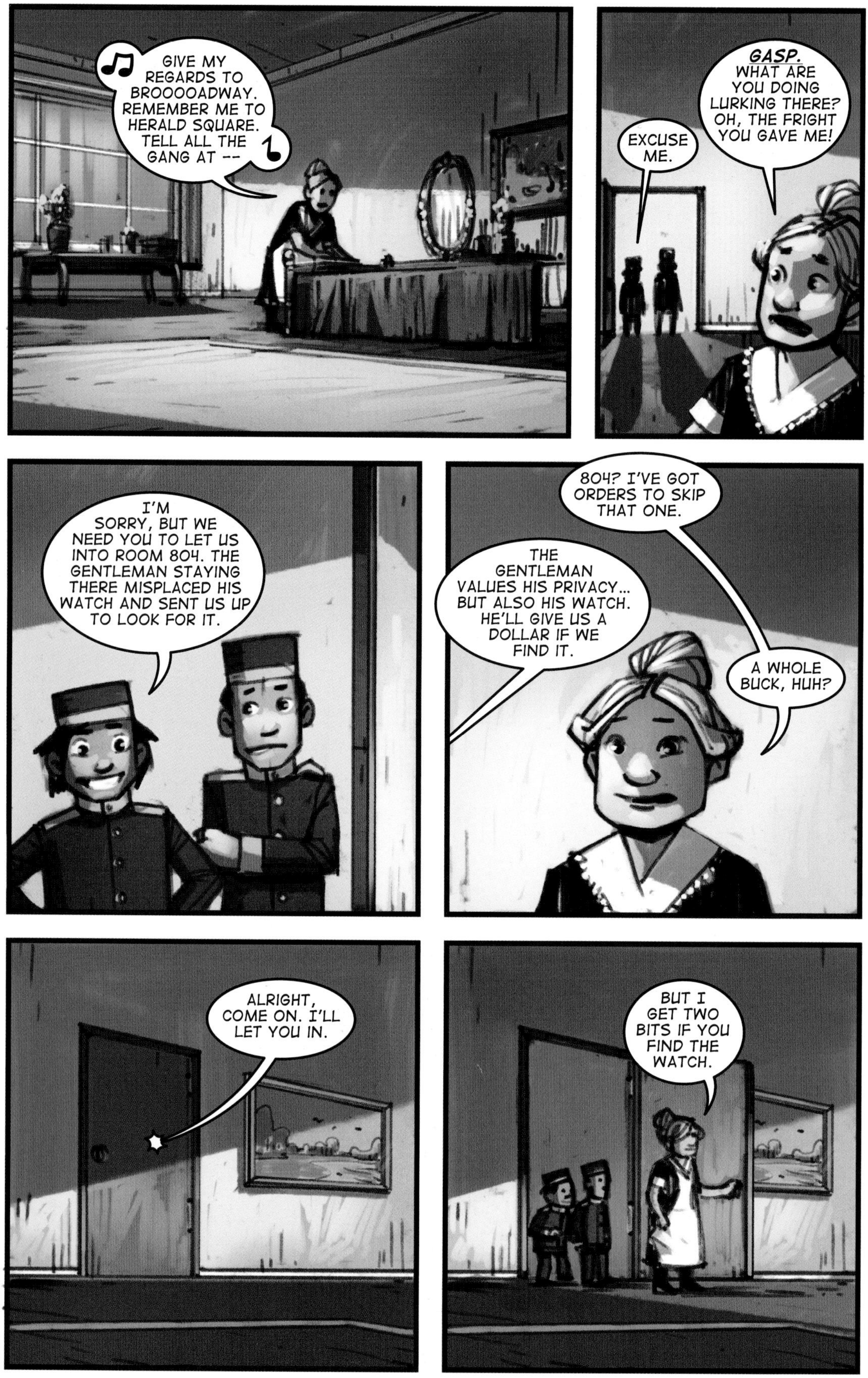
GIVE MY REGARDS TO BROOOOADWAY. REMEMBER ME TO HERALD SQUARE. TELL ALL THE GANG AT --
EXCUSE ME.
GASP. WHAT ARE YOU DOING LURKING THERE? OH, THE FRIGHT YOU GAVE ME!
I'M SORRY, BUT WE NEED YOU TO LET US INTO ROOM 804. THE GENTLEMAN STAYING THERE MISPLACED HIS WATCH AND SENT US UP TO LOOK FOR IT.
804? I'VE GOT ORDERS TO SKIP THAT ONE.
THE GENTLEMAN VALUES HIS PRIVACY... BUT ALSO HIS WATCH. HE'LL GIVE US A DOLLAR IF WE FIND IT.
A WHOLE BUCK, HUH?
ALRIGHT, COME ON. I'LL LET YOU IN.
BUT I GET TWO BITS IF YOU FIND THE WATCH.

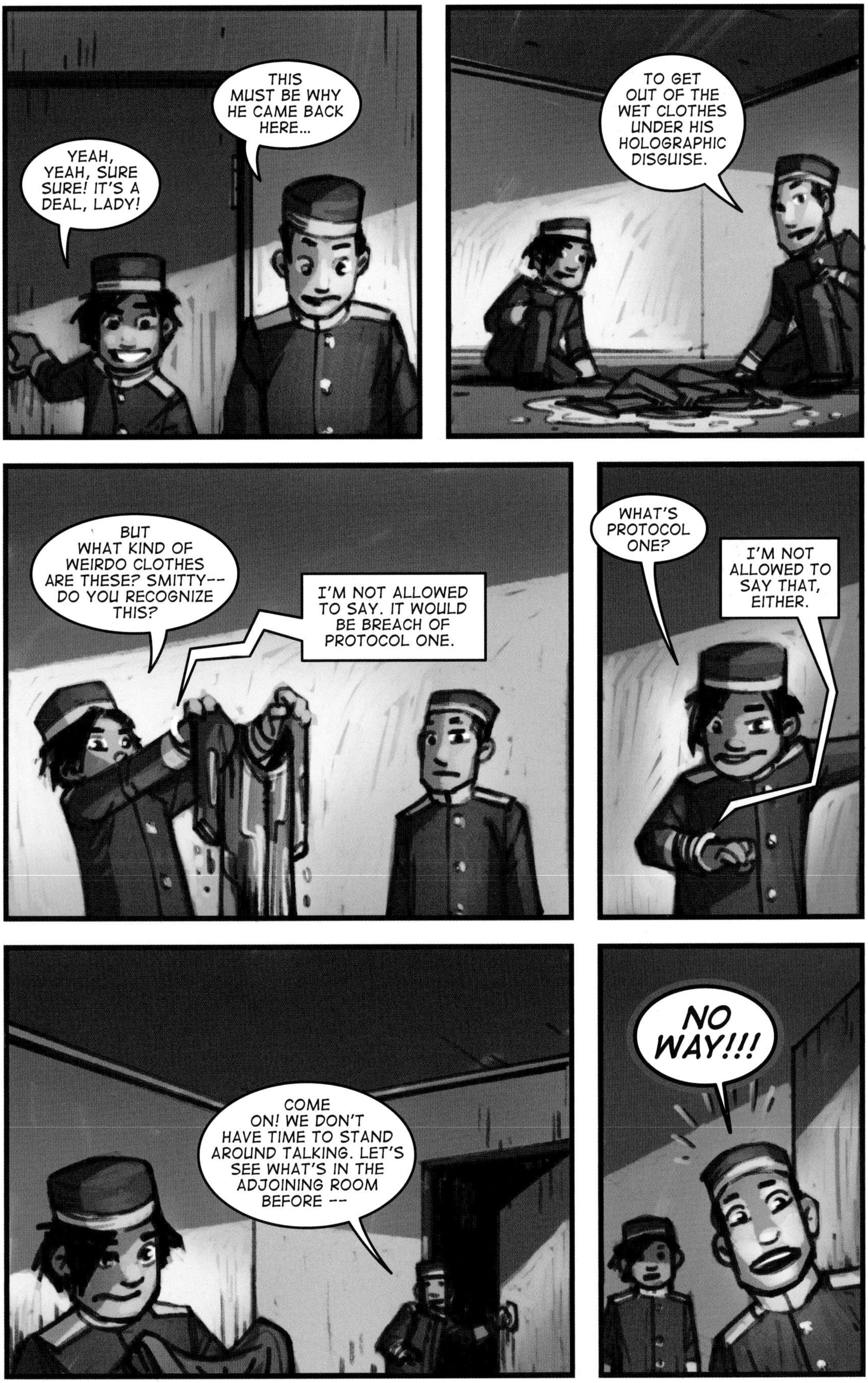
YEAH, YEAH, SURE SURE! IT'S A DEAL, LADY!
THIS MUST BE WHY HE CAME BACK HERE...
TO GET OUT OF THE WET CLOTHES UNDER HIS HOLOGRAPHIC DISGUISE.
BUT WHAT KIND OF WEIRDO CLOTHES ARE THESE? SMITTY-- DO YOU RECOGNIZE THIS?
I'M NOT ALLOWED TO SAY. IT WOULD BE BREACH OF PROTOCOL ONE.
WHAT'S PROTOCOL ONE?
I'M NOT ALLOWED TO SAY THAT, EITHER.
COME ON! WE DON'T HAVE TIME TO STAND AROUND TALKING. LET'S SEE WHAT'S IN THE ADJOINING ROOM BEFORE --
NO WAY!!!

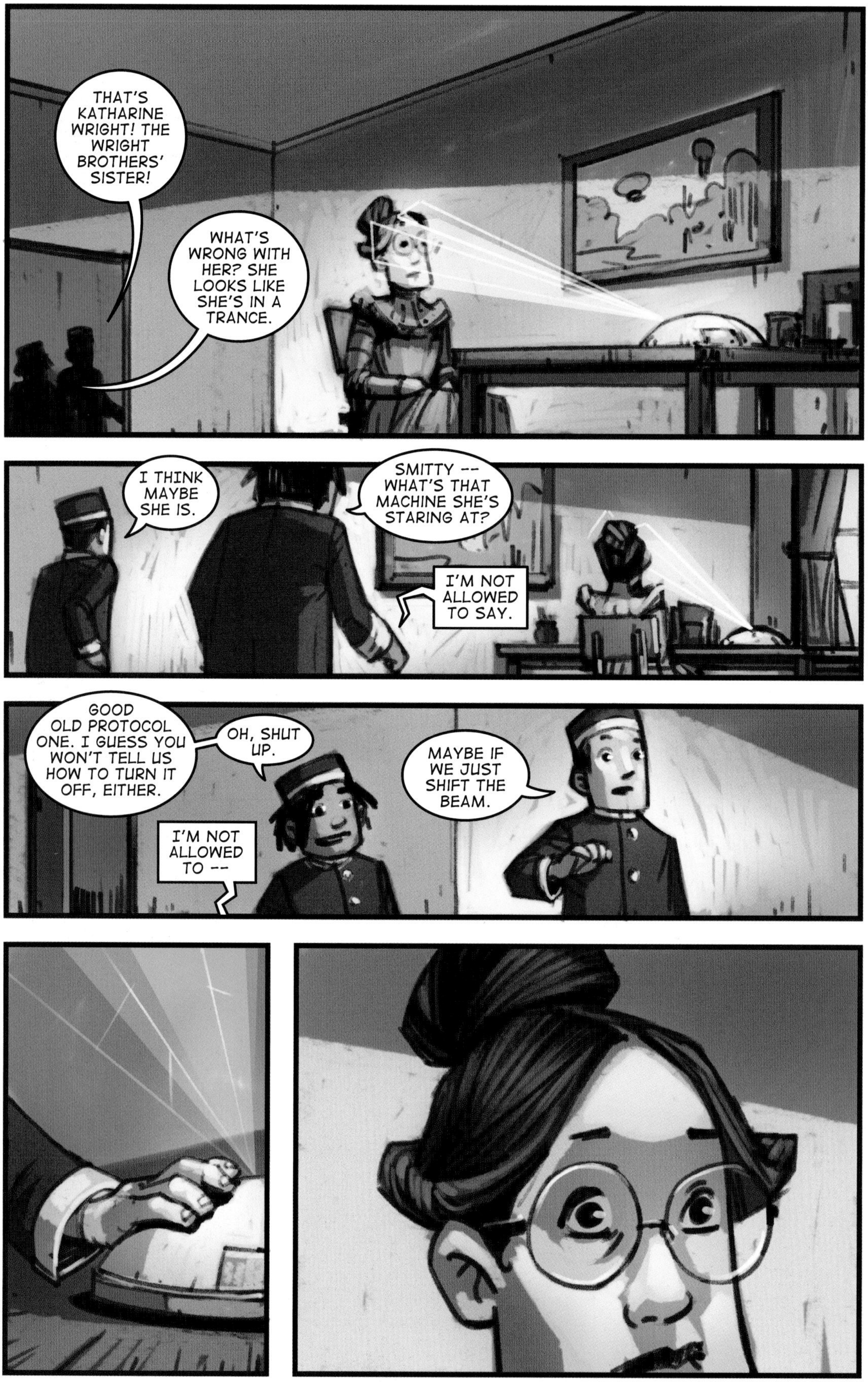
THAT'S KATHARINE WRIGHT! THE WRIGHT BROTHERS' SISTER!
WHAT'S WRONG WITH HER? SHE LOOKS LIKE SHE'S IN A TRANCE.
I THINK MAYBE SHE IS.
SMITTY -- WHAT'S THAT MACHINE SHE'S STARING AT?
I'M NOT ALLOWED TO SAY.
GOOD OLD PROTOCOL ONE. I GUESS YOU WON'T TELL US HOW TO TURN IT OFF, EITHER.
I'M NOT ALLOWED TO --
OH, SHUT UP.
MAYBE IF WE JUST SHIFT THE BEAM.

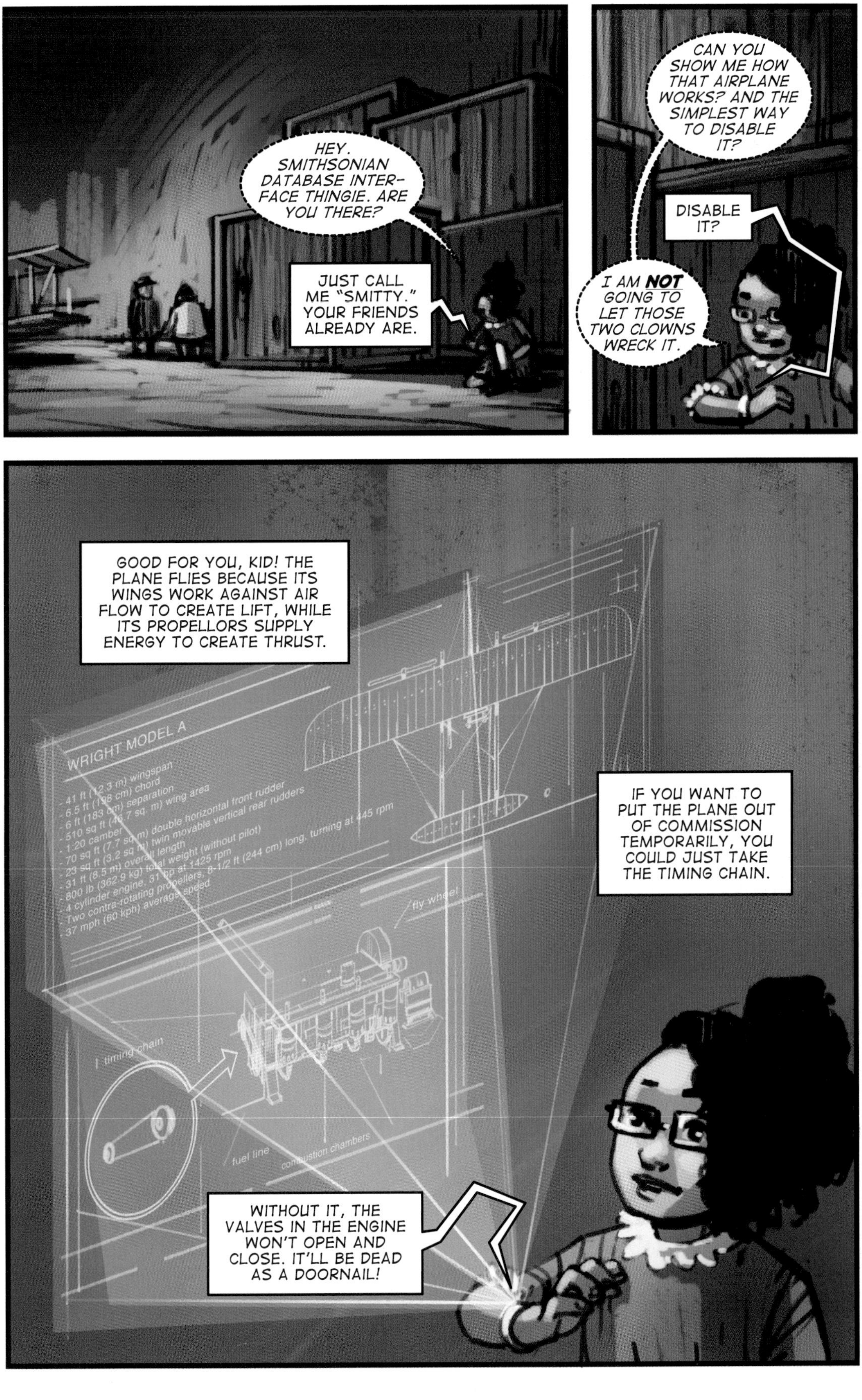
HEY. SMITHSONIAN DATABASE INTER-FACE THINGIE. ARE YOU THERE?
JUST CALL ME "SMITTY." YOUR FRIENDS ALREADY ARE.
CAN YOU SHOW ME HOW THAT AIRPLANE WORKS? AND THE SIMPLEST WAY TO DISABLE IT?
DISABLE IT?
I AM **NOT** GOING TO LET THOSE TWO CLOWNS WRECK IT.
GOOD FOR YOU, KID! THE PLANE FLIES BECAUSE ITS WINGS WORK AGAINST AIR FLOW TO CREATE LIFT, WHILE ITS PROPELLORS SUPPLY ENERGY TO CREATE THRUST.
WRIGHT MODEL A
- 41 ft (12.3 m) wingspan
- 6.5 ft (198 cm) chord
- 6 ft (183 cm) separation
- 510 sq ft (46.7 sq. m) wing area
- 1:20 camber
- 70 sq ft (7.7 sq m) double horizontal front rudder
- 23 sq ft (3.2 sq m) twin movable vertical rear rudders
- 31 ft (8.5 m) overall length
- 800 lb (362.9 kg) total weight (without pilot)
- 4 cylinder engine, 31 hp at 1425 rpm
- Two contra-rotating propellers, 8-1/2 ft (244 cm) long, turning at 445 rpm
- 37 mph (60 kph) average speed
fly wheel
timing chain
fuel line
combustion chambers
IF YOU WANT TO PUT THE PLANE OUT OF COMMISSION TEMPORARILY, YOU COULD JUST TAKE THE TIMING CHAIN.
WITHOUT IT, THE VALVES IN THE ENGINE WON'T OPEN AND CLOSE. IT'LL BE DEAD AS A DOORNAIL!

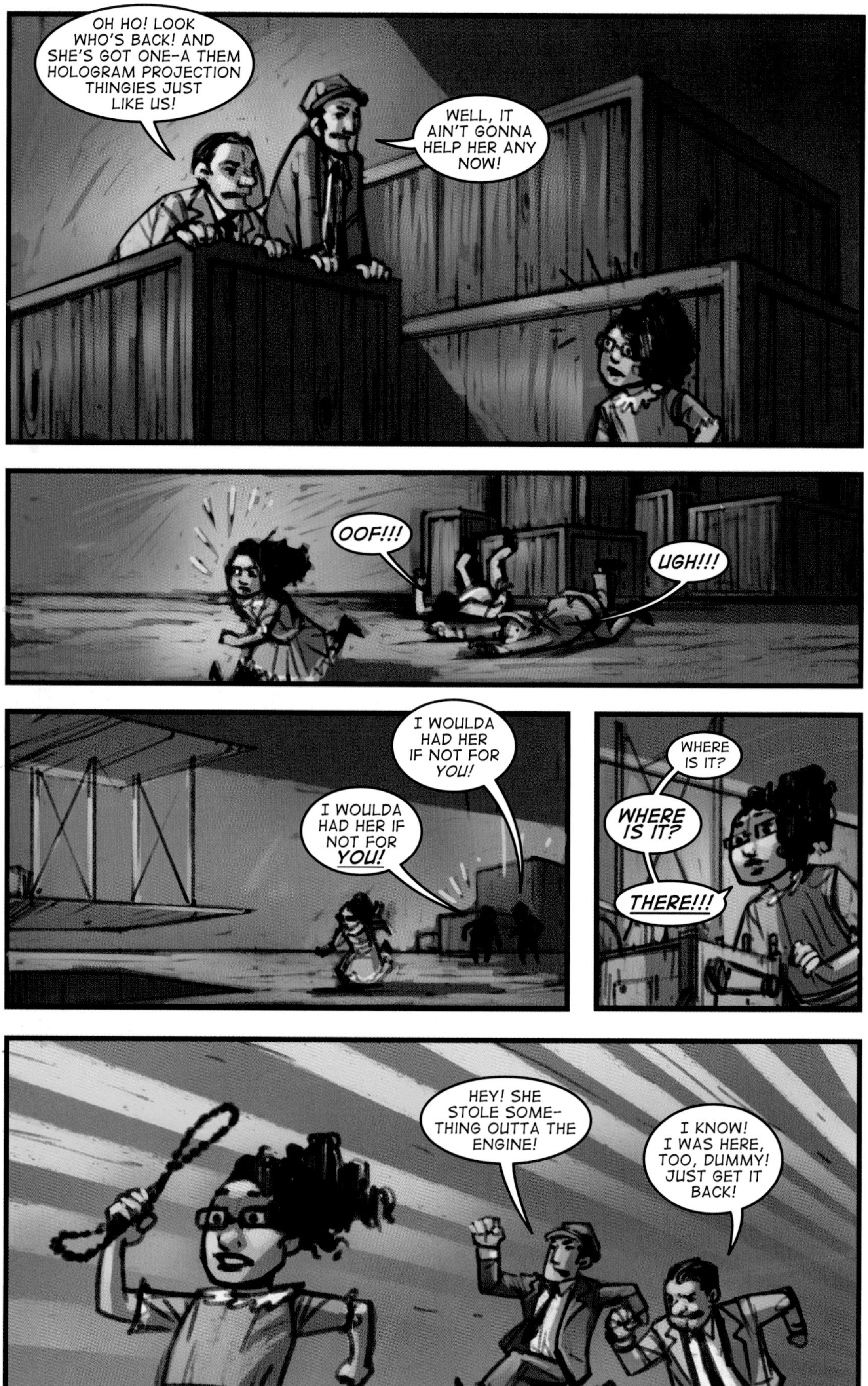
OH HO! LOOK WHO'S BACK! AND SHE'S GOT ONE-A THEM HOLOGRAM PROJECTION THINGIES JUST LIKE US!
WELL, IT AIN'T GONNA HELP HER ANY NOW!
OOF!!!
UGH!!!
I WOULDA HAD HER IF NOT FOR YOU!
I WOULDA HAD HER IF NOT FOR YOU!
WHERE IS IT?
WHERE IS IT?
THERE!!!
HEY! SHE STOLE SOME-THING OUTTA THE ENGINE!
I KNOW! I WAS HERE, TOO, DUMMY! JUST GET IT BACK!

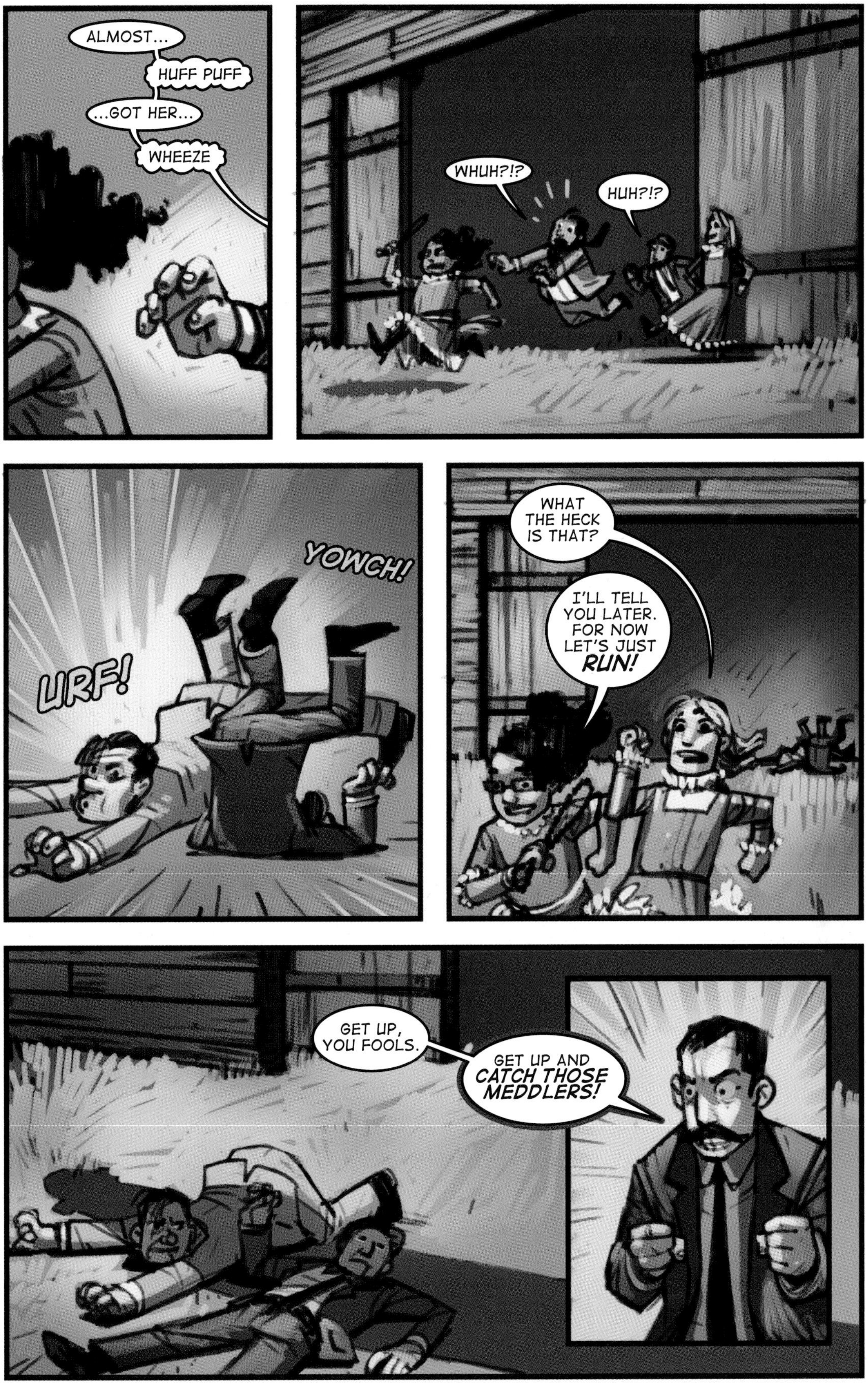
ALMOST...
HUFF PUFF
...GOT HER...
WHEEZE
WHUH?!?
HUH?!?
YOWCH!
URF!
WHAT THE HECK IS THAT?
I'LL TELL YOU LATER. FOR NOW LET'S JUST RUN!
GET UP, YOU FOOLS.
GET UP AND CATCH THOSE MEDDLERS!

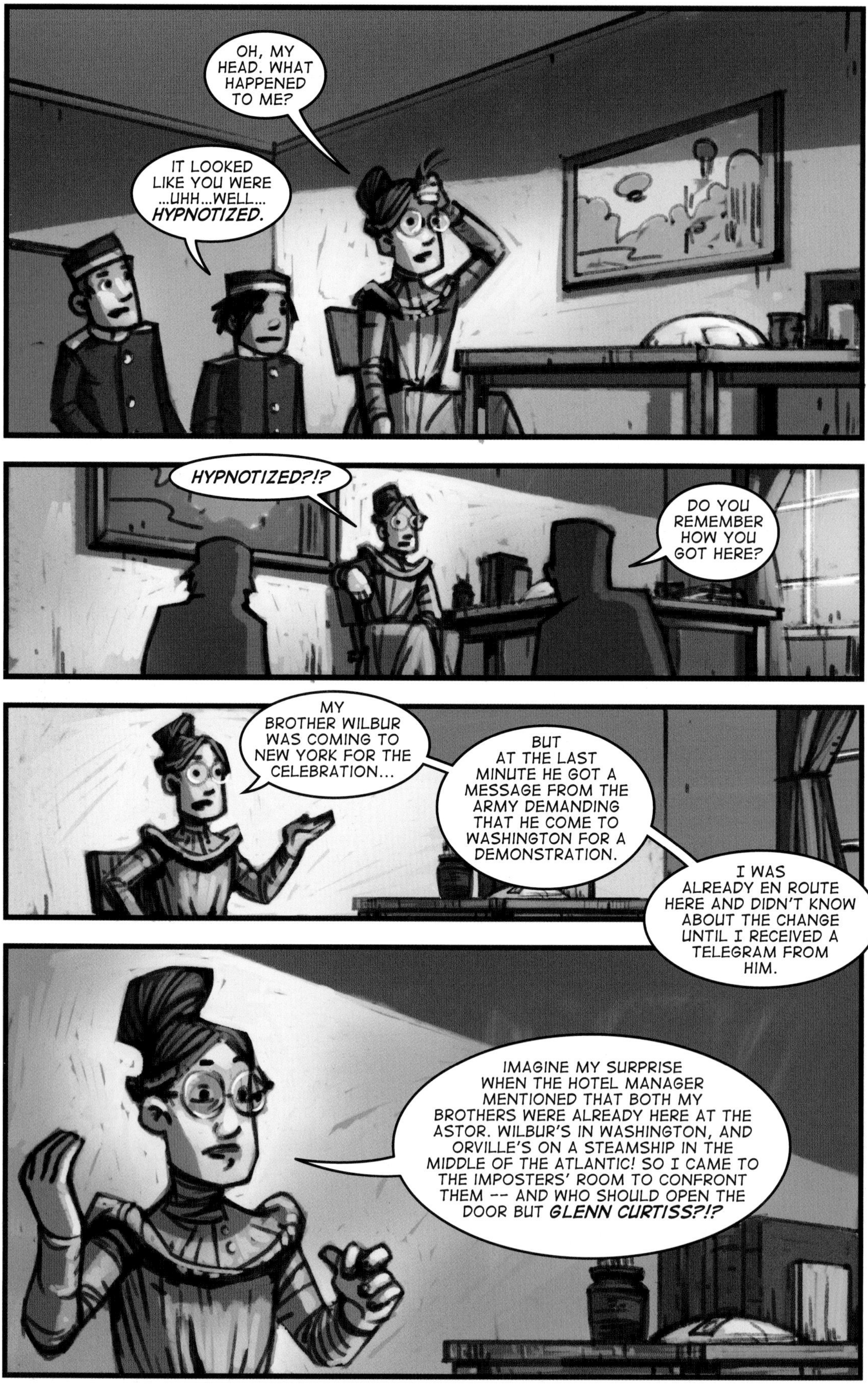

OH, MY HEAD. WHAT HAPPENED TO ME?
IT LOOKED LIKE YOU WERE ...UHH...WELL... HYPNOTIZED.
HYPNOTIZED?!?
DO YOU REMEMBER HOW YOU GOT HERE?
MY BROTHER WILBUR WAS COMING TO NEW YORK FOR THE CELEBRATION...
BUT AT THE LAST MINUTE HE GOT A MESSAGE FROM THE ARMY DEMANDING THAT HE COME TO WASHINGTON FOR A DEMONSTRATION.
I WAS ALREADY EN ROUTE HERE AND DIDN'T KNOW ABOUT THE CHANGE UNTIL I RECEIVED A TELEGRAM FROM HIM.
IMAGINE MY SURPRISE WHEN THE HOTEL MANAGER MENTIONED THAT BOTH MY BROTHERS WERE ALREADY HERE AT THE ASTOR. WILBUR'S IN WASHINGTON, AND ORVILLE'S ON A STEAMSHIP IN THE MIDDLE OF THE ATLANTIC! SO I CAME TO THE IMPOSTERS' ROOM TO CONFRONT THEM -- AND WHO SHOULD OPEN THE DOOR BUT GLENN CURTISS?!?

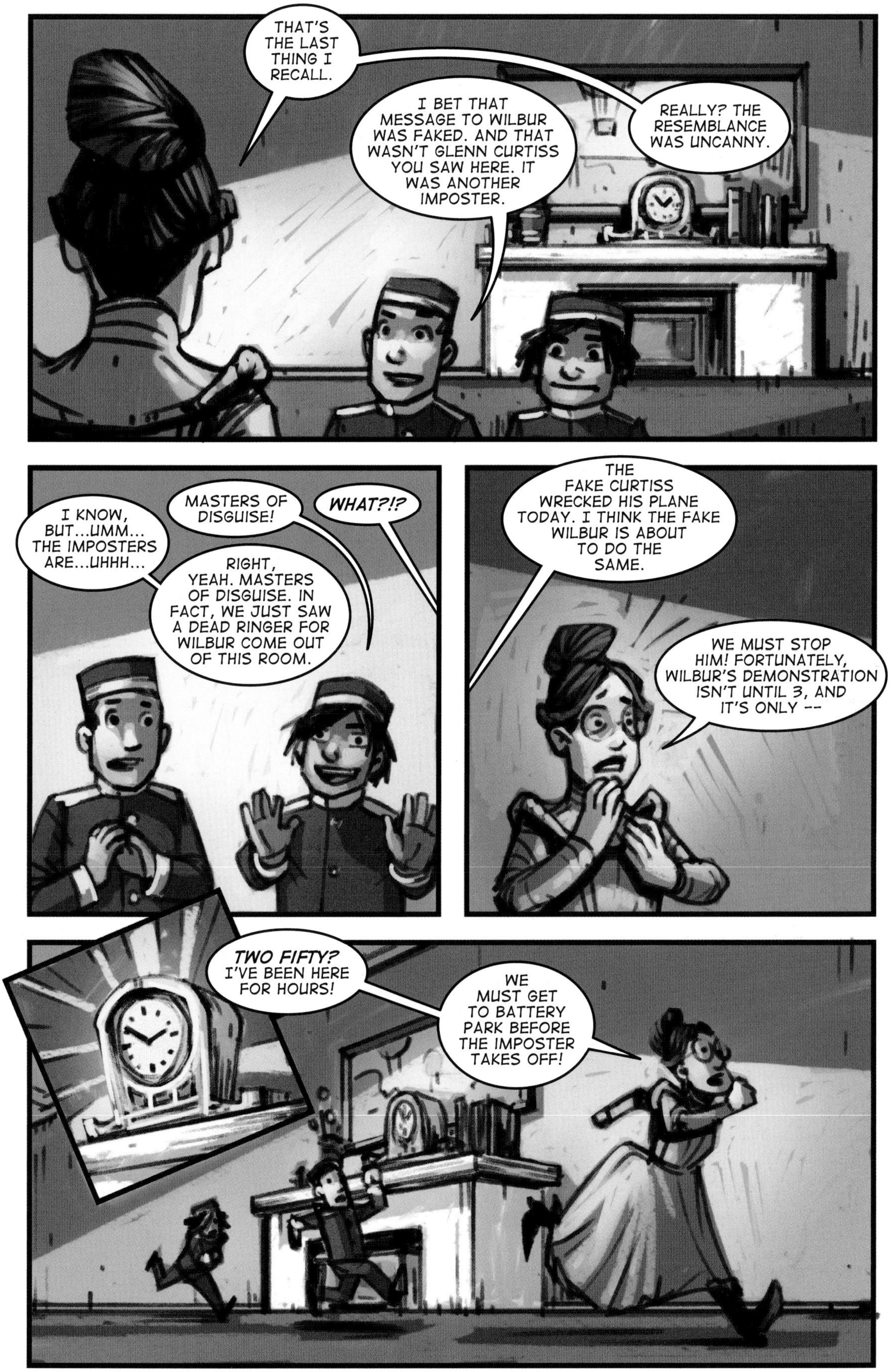
THAT'S THE LAST THING I RECALL.
REALLY? THE RESEMBLANCE WAS UNCANNY.
I BET THAT MESSAGE TO WILBUR WAS FAKED. AND THAT WASN'T GLENN CURTISS YOU SAW HERE. IT WAS ANOTHER IMPOSTER.
I KNOW, BUT...UMM... THE IMPOSTERS ARE...UHHH...
MASTERS OF DISGUISE!
WHAT?!?
RIGHT, YEAH. MASTERS OF DISGUISE. IN FACT, WE JUST SAW A DEAD RINGER FOR WILBUR COME OUT OF THIS ROOM.
THE FAKE CURTISS WRECKED HIS PLANE TODAY. I THINK THE FAKE WILBUR IS ABOUT TO DO THE SAME.
WE MUST STOP HIM! FORTUNATELY, WILBUR'S DEMONSTRATION ISN'T UNTIL 3, AND IT'S ONLY --
TWO FIFTY? I'VE BEEN HERE FOR HOURS!
WE MUST GET TO BATTERY PARK BEFORE THE IMPOSTER TAKES OFF!

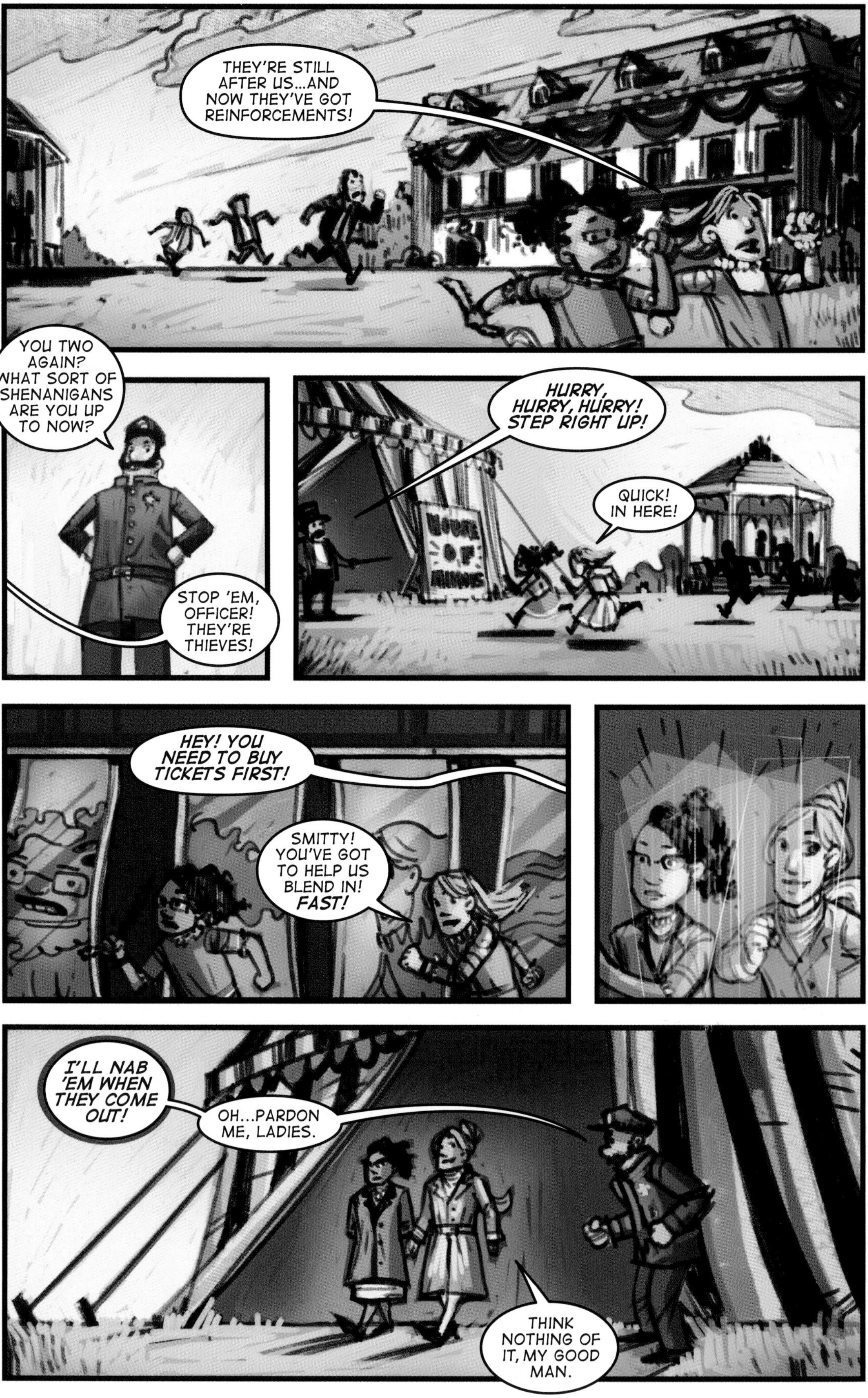
THEY'RE STILL AFTER US...AND NOW THEY'VE GOT REINFORCEMENTS!
YOU TWO AGAIN? WHAT SORT OF SHENANIGANS ARE YOU UP TO NOW?
STOP 'EM, OFFICER! THEY'RE THIEVES!
HURRY, HURRY, HURRY! STEP RIGHT UP!
QUICK! IN HERE!
HEY! YOU NEED TO BUY TICKETS FIRST!
SMITTY! YOU'VE GOT TO HELP US BLEND IN! FAST!
I'LL NAB 'EM WHEN THEY COME OUT!
OH...PARDON ME, LADIES.
THINK NOTHING OF IT, MY GOOD MAN.

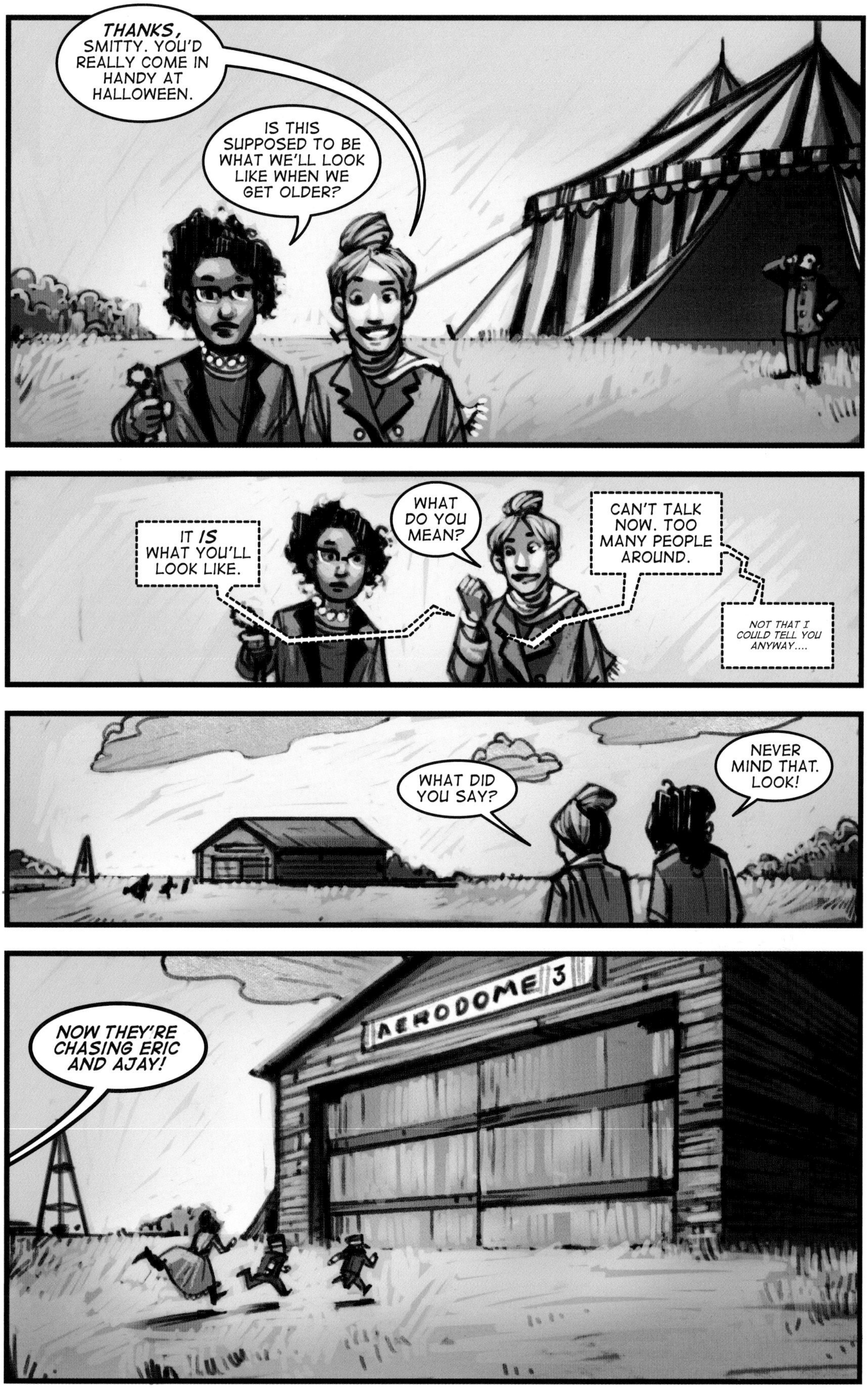
THANKS, SMITTY. YOU'D REALLY COME IN HANDY AT HALLOWEEN.
IS THIS SUPPOSED TO BE WHAT WE'LL LOOK LIKE WHEN WE GET OLDER?
IT IS WHAT YOU'LL LOOK LIKE.
WHAT DO YOU MEAN?
CAN'T TALK NOW. TOO MANY PEOPLE AROUND.
NOT THAT I COULD TELL YOU ANYWAY....
WHAT DID YOU SAY?
NEVER MIND THAT. LOOK!
AERODOME 3
NOW THEY'RE CHASING ERIC AND AJAY!

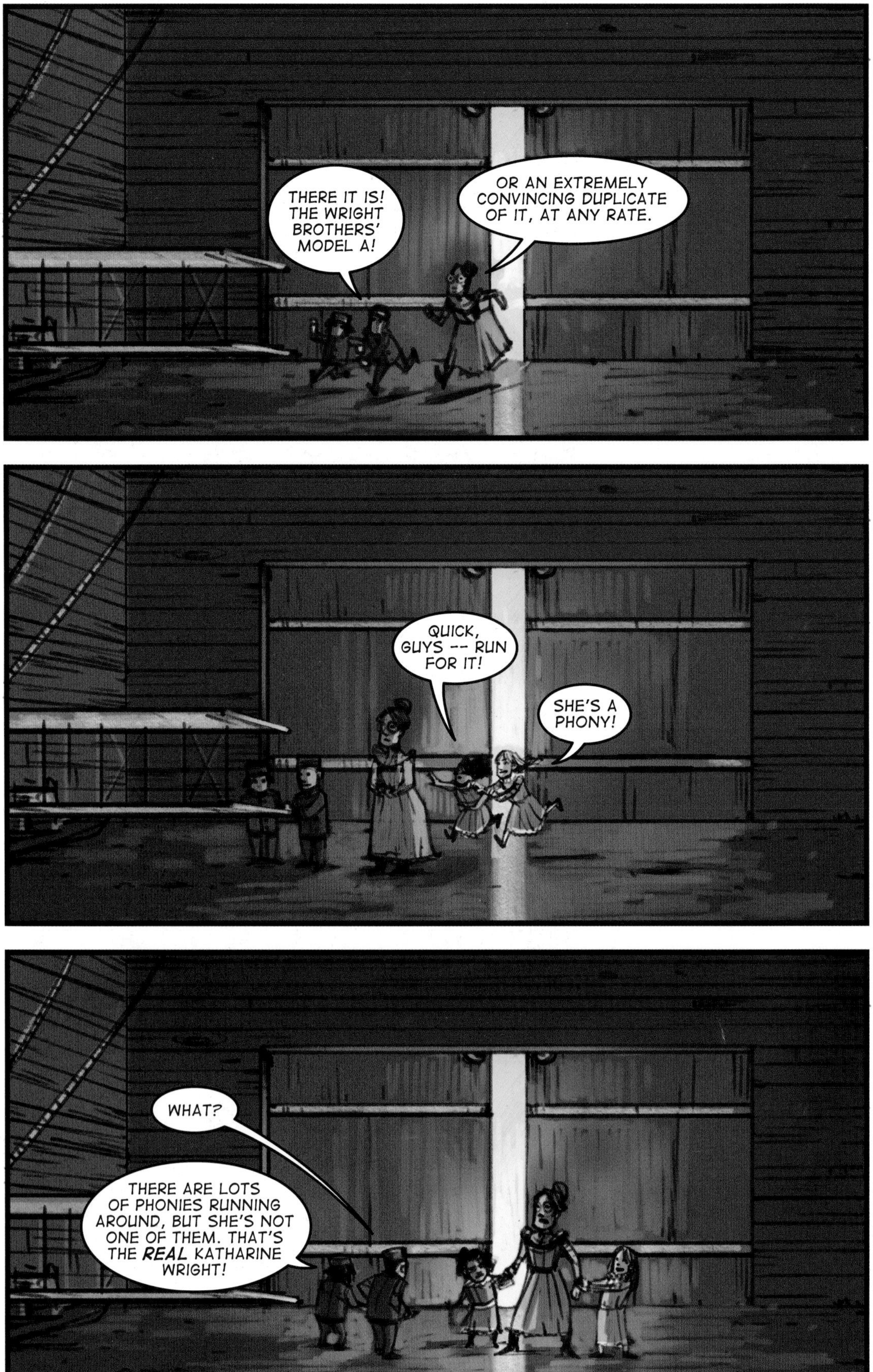
THERE IT IS! THE WRIGHT BROTHERS' MODEL A!
OR AN EXTREMELY CONVINCING DUPLICATE OF IT, AT ANY RATE.
QUICK, GUYS -- RUN FOR IT!
SHE'S A PHONY!
WHAT?
THERE ARE LOTS OF PHONIES RUNNING AROUND, BUT SHE'S NOT ONE OF THEM. THAT'S THE *REAL* KATHARINE WRIGHT!

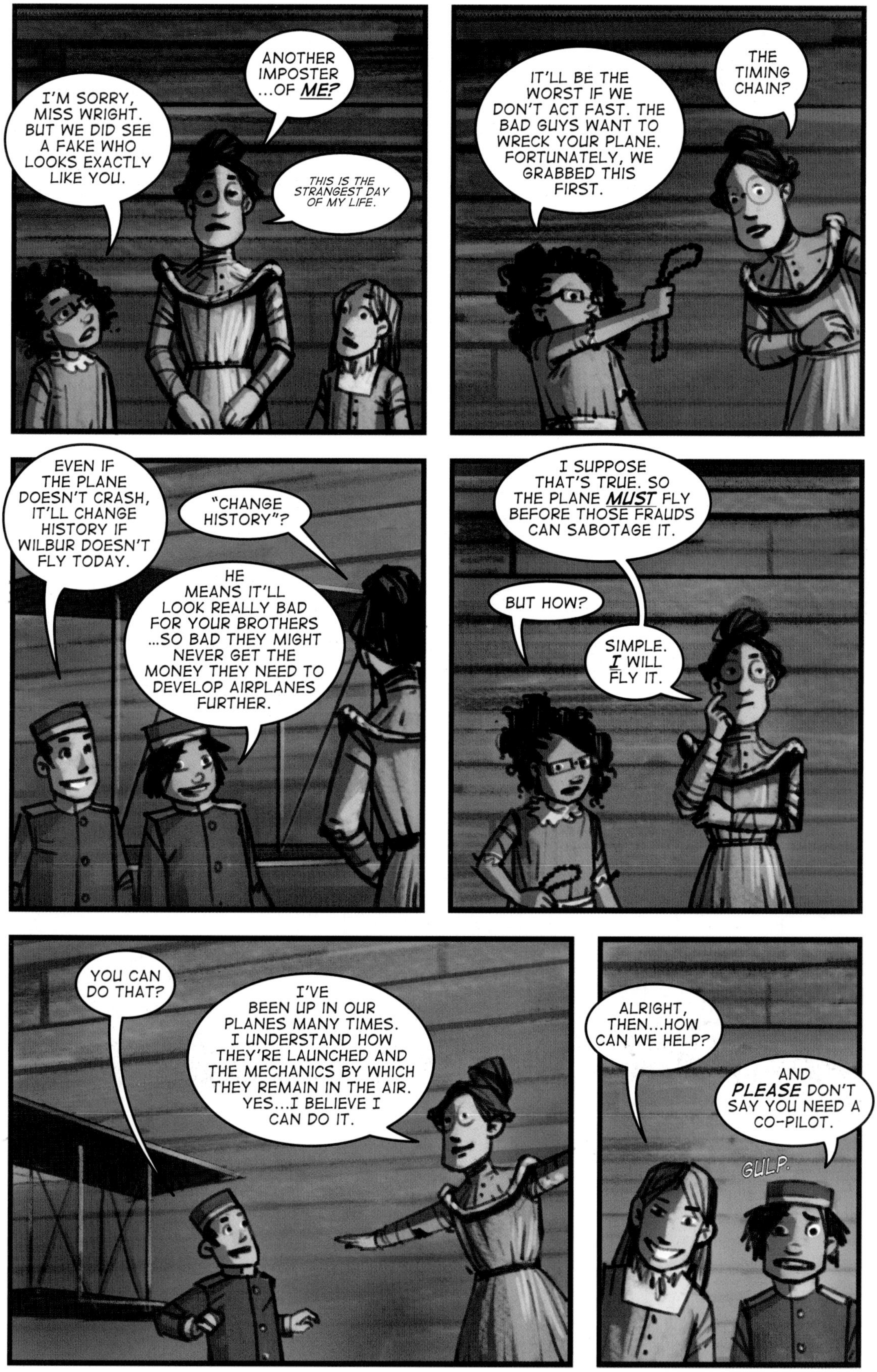
I'M SORRY, MISS WRIGHT. BUT WE DID SEE A FAKE WHO LOOKS EXACTLY LIKE YOU.
ANOTHER IMPOSTER ...OF ME?
THIS IS THE STRANGEST DAY OF MY LIFE.
IT'LL BE THE WORST IF WE DON'T ACT FAST. THE BAD GUYS WANT TO WRECK YOUR PLANE. FORTUNATELY, WE GRABBED THIS FIRST.
THE TIMING CHAIN?
EVEN IF THE PLANE DOESN'T CRASH, IT'LL CHANGE HISTORY IF WILBUR DOESN'T FLY TODAY.
"CHANGE HISTORY"?
HE MEANS IT'LL LOOK REALLY BAD FOR YOUR BROTHERS ...SO BAD THEY MIGHT NEVER GET THE MONEY THEY NEED TO DEVELOP AIRPLANES FURTHER.
I SUPPOSE THAT'S TRUE. SO THE PLANE MUST FLY BEFORE THOSE FRAUDS CAN SABOTAGE IT.
BUT HOW?
SIMPLE. I WILL FLY IT.
YOU CAN DO THAT?
I'VE BEEN UP IN OUR PLANES MANY TIMES. I UNDERSTAND HOW THEY'RE LAUNCHED AND THE MECHANICS BY WHICH THEY REMAIN IN THE AIR. YES...I BELIEVE I CAN DO IT.
ALRIGHT, THEN...HOW CAN WE HELP?
AND PLEASE DON'T SAY YOU NEED A CO-PILOT.
GULP.

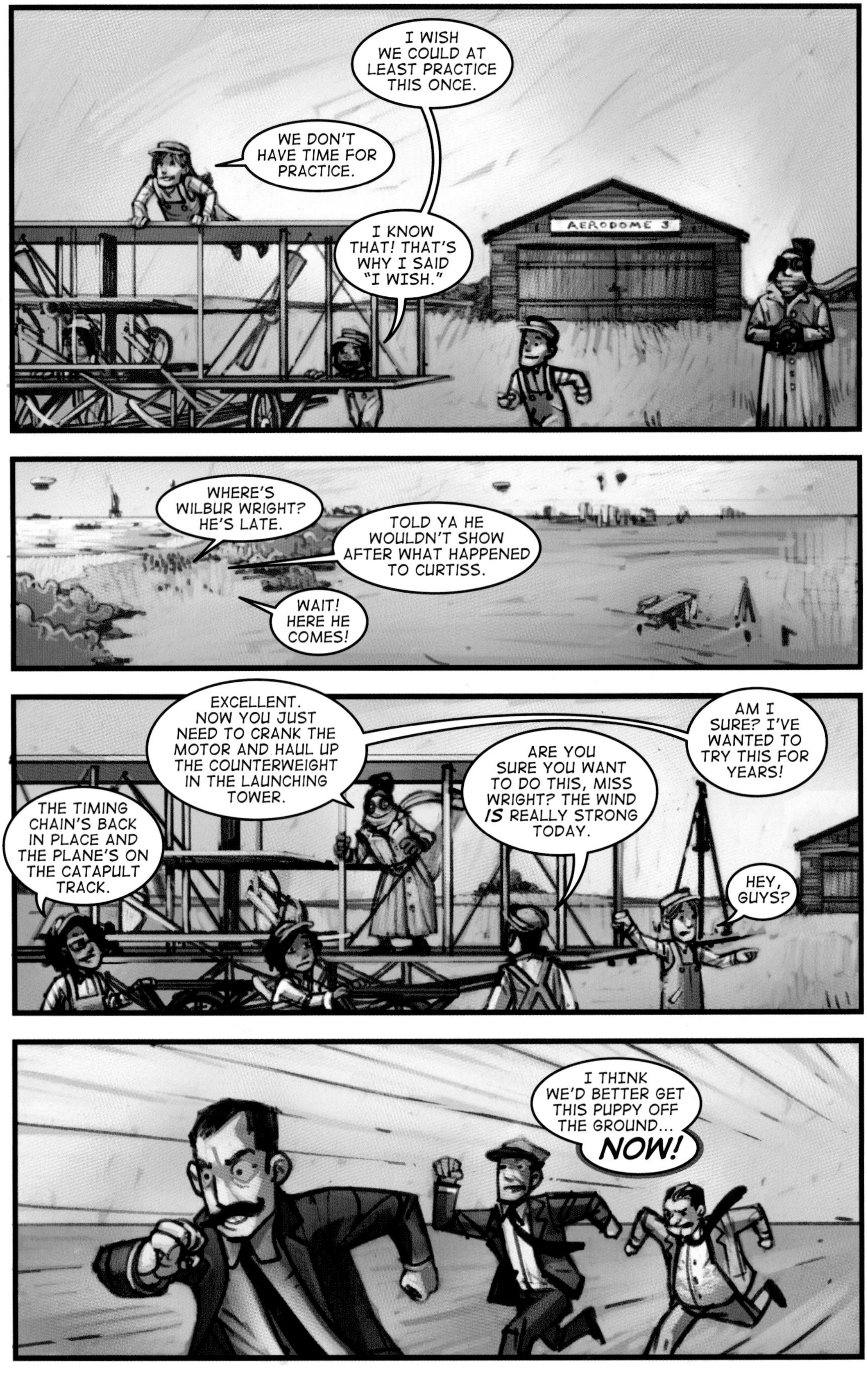
I WISH WE COULD AT LEAST PRACTICE THIS ONCE.
WE DON'T HAVE TIME FOR PRACTICE.
I KNOW THAT! THAT'S WHY I SAID "I WISH."
AERODOME 3
WHERE'S WILBUR WRIGHT? HE'S LATE.
TOLD YA HE WOULDN'T SHOW AFTER WHAT HAPPENED TO CURTISS.
WAIT! HERE HE COMES!
THE TIMING CHAIN'S BACK IN PLACE AND THE PLANE'S ON THE CATAPULT TRACK.
EXCELLENT. NOW YOU JUST NEED TO CRANK THE MOTOR AND HAUL UP THE COUNTERWEIGHT IN THE LAUNCHING TOWER.
ARE YOU SURE YOU WANT TO DO THIS, MISS WRIGHT? THE WIND *IS* REALLY STRONG TODAY.
AM I SURE? I'VE WANTED TO TRY THIS FOR YEARS!
HEY, GUYS?
I THINK WE'D BETTER GET THIS PUPPY OFF THE GROUND... **NOW!**

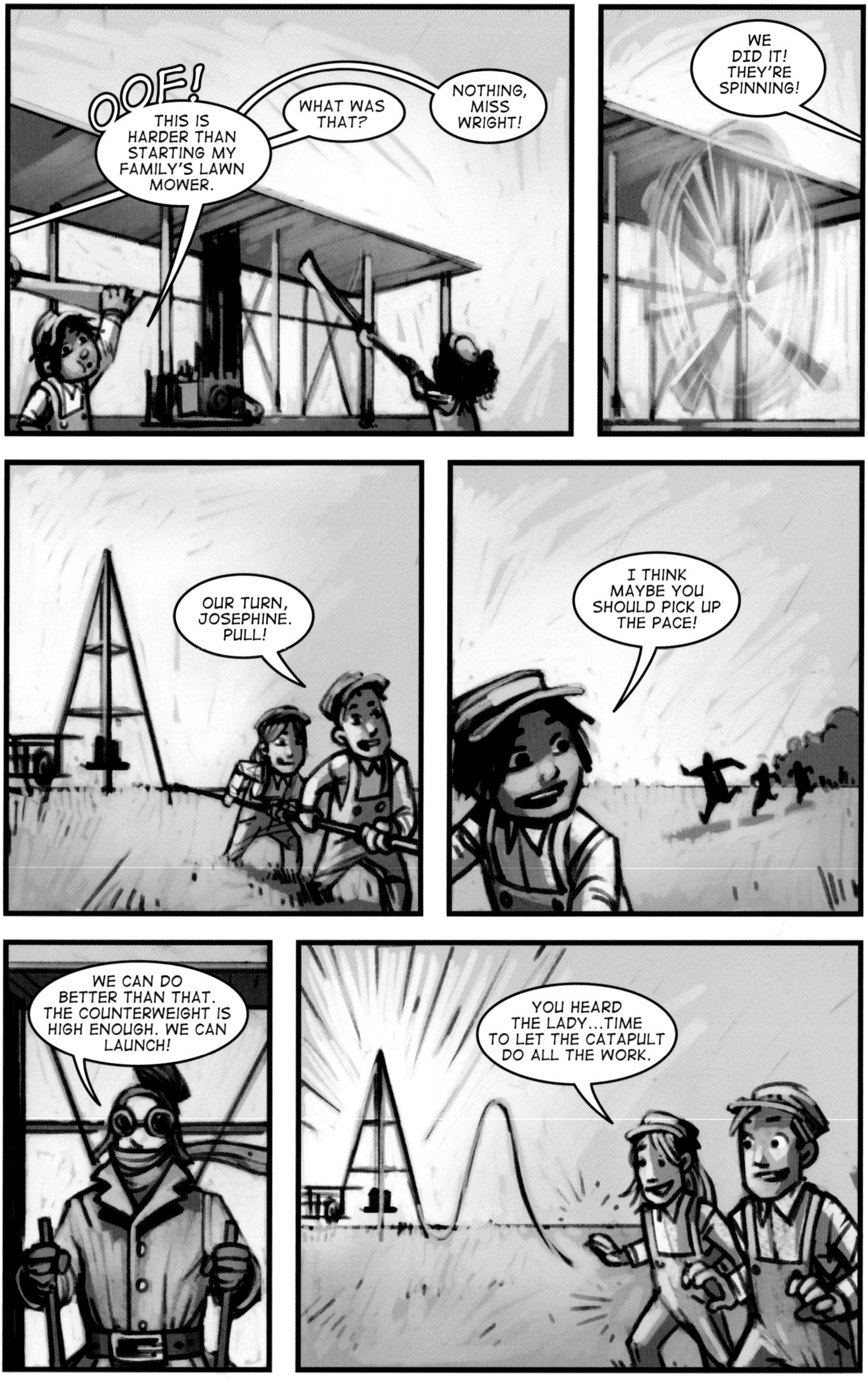
OOF!
THIS IS HARDER THAN STARTING MY FAMILY'S LAWN MOWER.
WHAT WAS THAT?
NOTHING, MISS WRIGHT!
WE DID IT! THEY'RE SPINNING!
OUR TURN, JOSEPHINE. PULL!
I THINK MAYBE YOU SHOULD PICK UP THE PACE!
WE CAN DO BETTER THAN THAT. THE COUNTERWEIGHT IS HIGH ENOUGH. WE CAN LAUNCH!
YOU HEARD THE LADY...TIME TO LET THE CATAPULT DO ALL THE WORK.

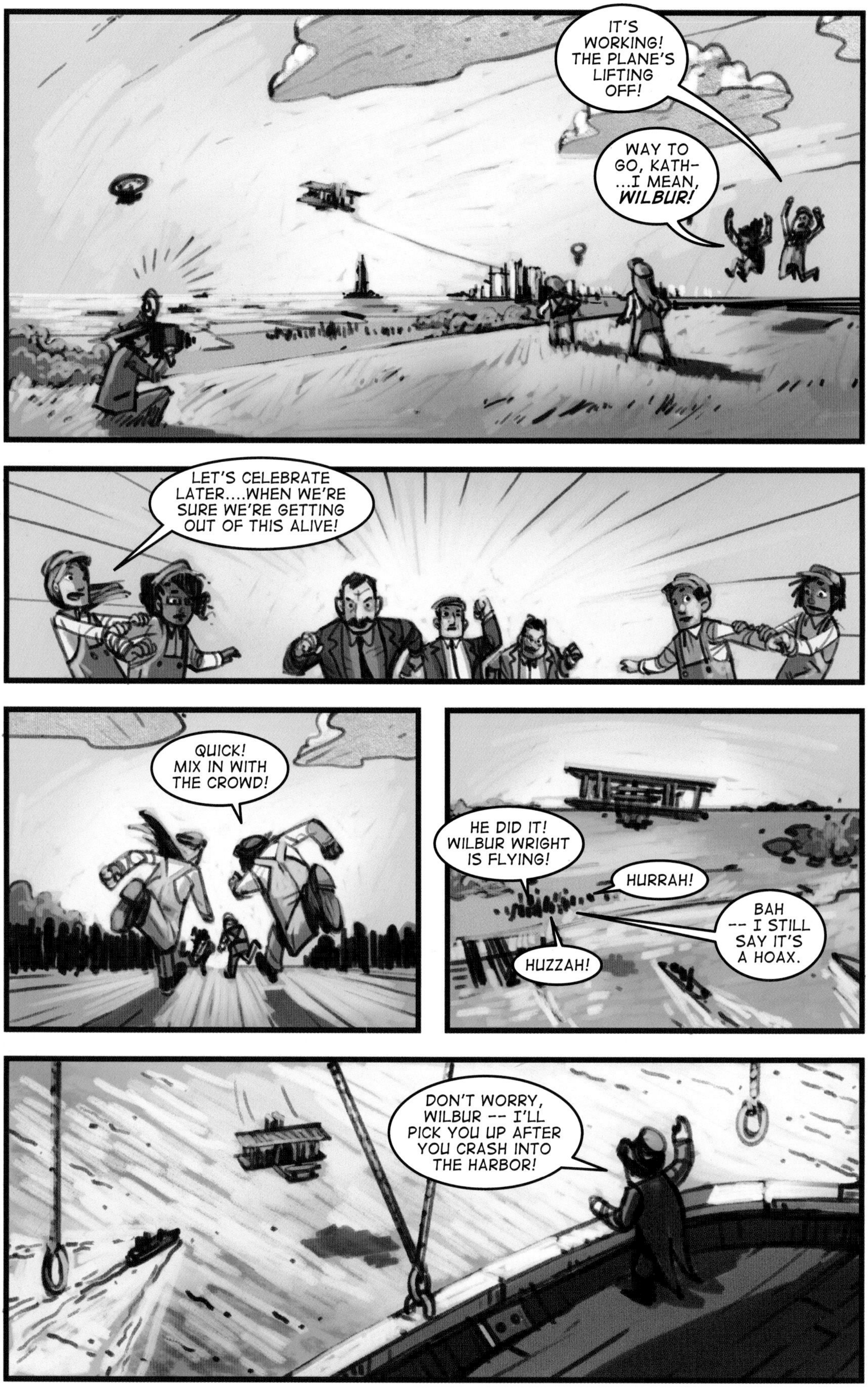
IT'S WORKING! THE PLANE'S LIFTING OFF!
WAY TO GO, KATH- ...I MEAN, WILBUR!
LET'S CELEBRATE LATER....WHEN WE'RE SURE WE'RE GETTING OUT OF THIS ALIVE!
QUICK! MIX IN WITH THE CROWD!
HE DID IT! WILBUR WRIGHT IS FLYING!
HURRAH!
BAH -- I STILL SAY IT'S A HOAX.
HUZZAH!
DON'T WORRY, WILBUR -- I'LL PICK YOU UP AFTER YOU CRASH INTO THE HARBOR!

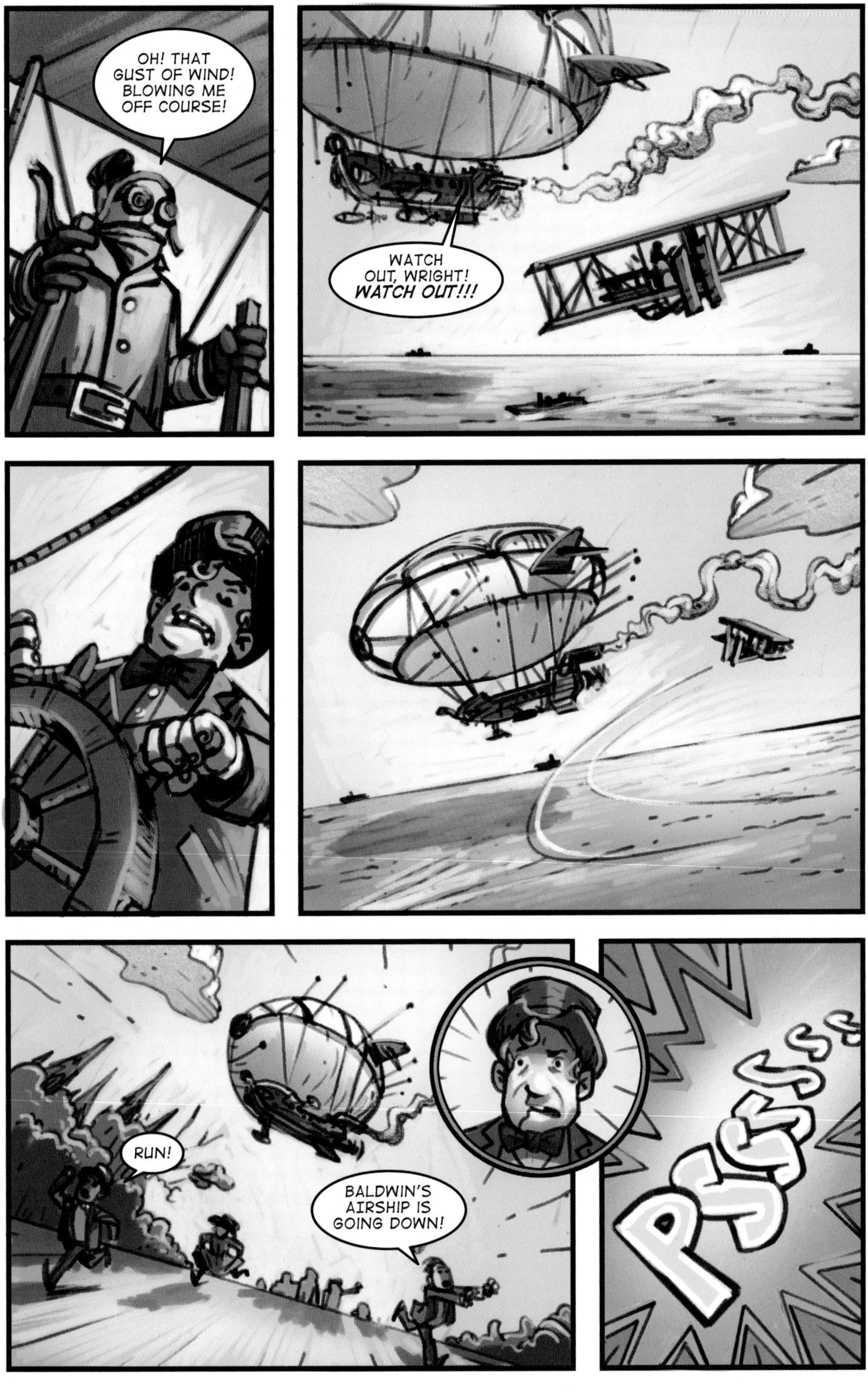
OH! THAT GUST OF WIND! BLOWING ME OFF COURSE!
WATCH OUT, WRIGHT! WATCH OUT!!!
RUN!
BALDWIN'S AIRSHIP IS GOING DOWN!
PSSSSS

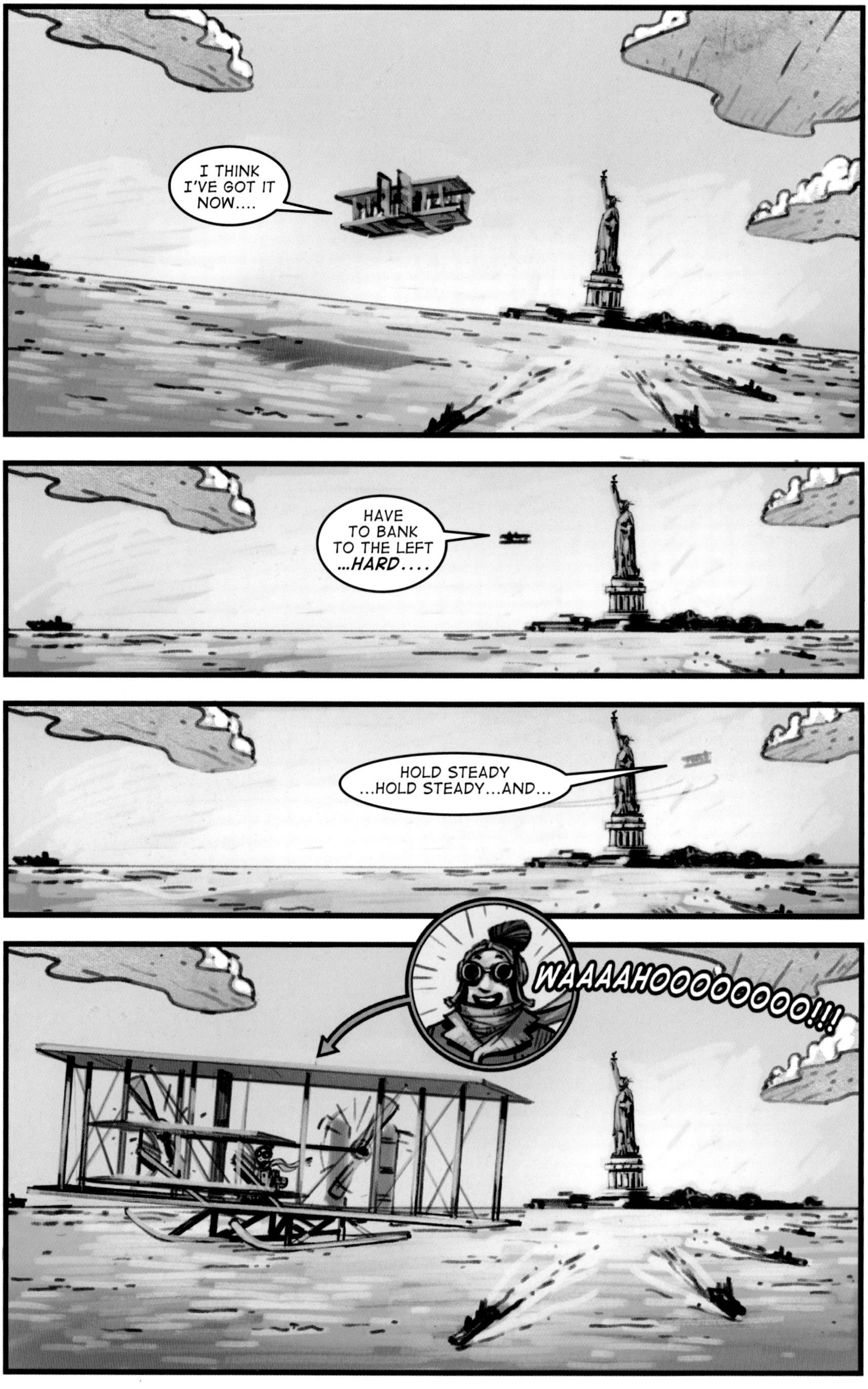
I THINK I'VE GOT IT NOW....
HAVE TO BANK TO THE LEFT ...HARD....
HOLD STEADY ...HOLD STEADY...AND...
WAAAAHOOOOOOOOO!!!

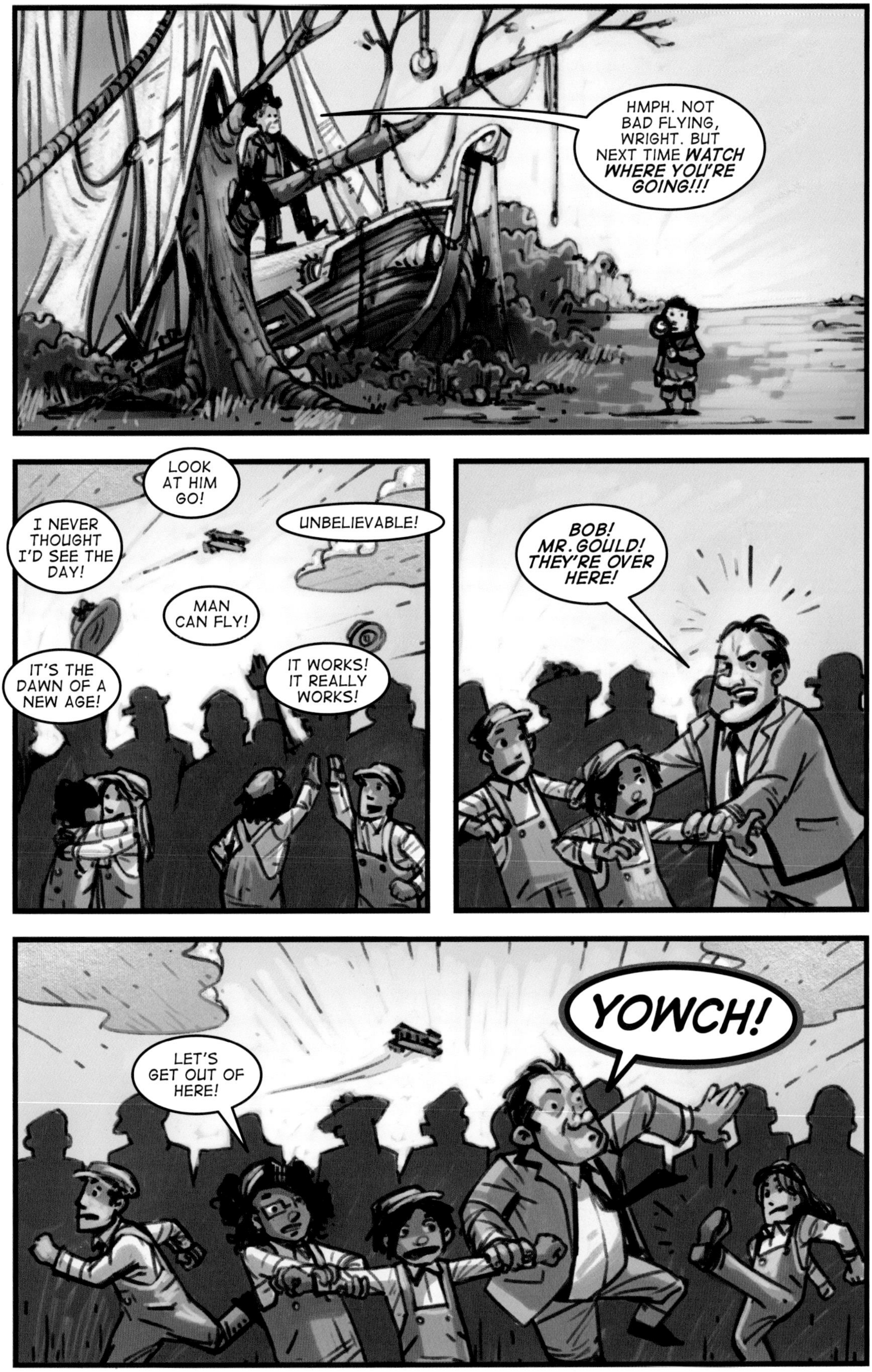
HMPH. NOT BAD FLYING, WRIGHT. BUT NEXT TIME WATCH WHERE YOU'RE GOING!!!
LOOK AT HIM GO!
I NEVER THOUGHT I'D SEE THE DAY!
UNBELIEVABLE!
MAN CAN FLY!
IT'S THE DAWN OF A NEW AGE!
IT WORKS! IT REALLY WORKS!
BOB! MR. GOULD! THEY'RE OVER HERE!
YOWCH!
LET'S GET OUT OF HERE!

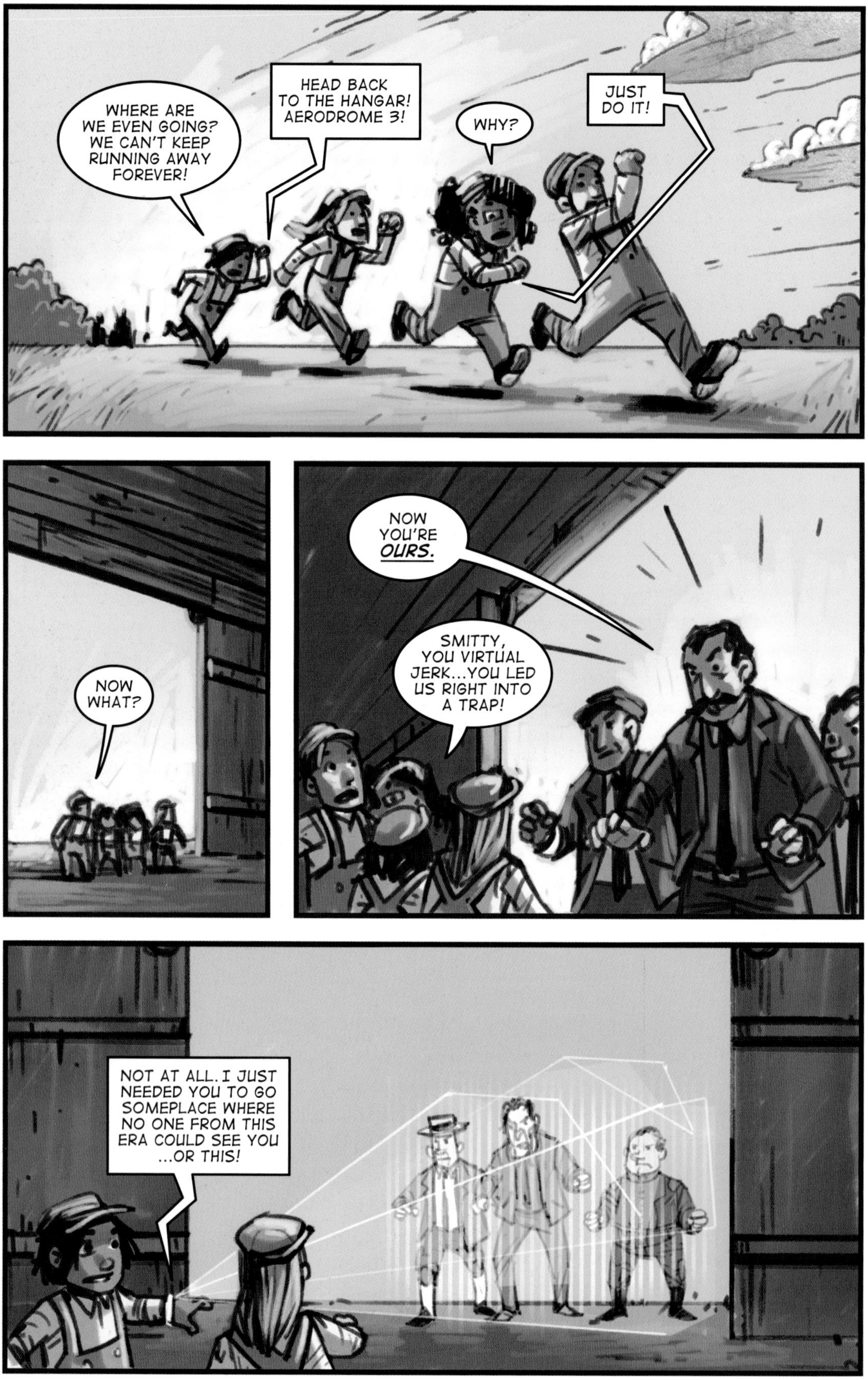
WHERE ARE WE EVEN GOING? WE CAN'T KEEP RUNNING AWAY FOREVER!
HEAD BACK TO THE HANGAR! AERODROME 3!
WHY?
JUST DO IT!
NOW WHAT?
NOW YOU'RE ***OURS.***
SMITTY, YOU VIRTUAL JERK...YOU LED US RIGHT INTO A TRAP!
NOT AT ALL. I JUST NEEDED YOU TO GO SOMEPLACE WHERE NO ONE FROM THIS ERA COULD SEE YOU ...OR THIS!

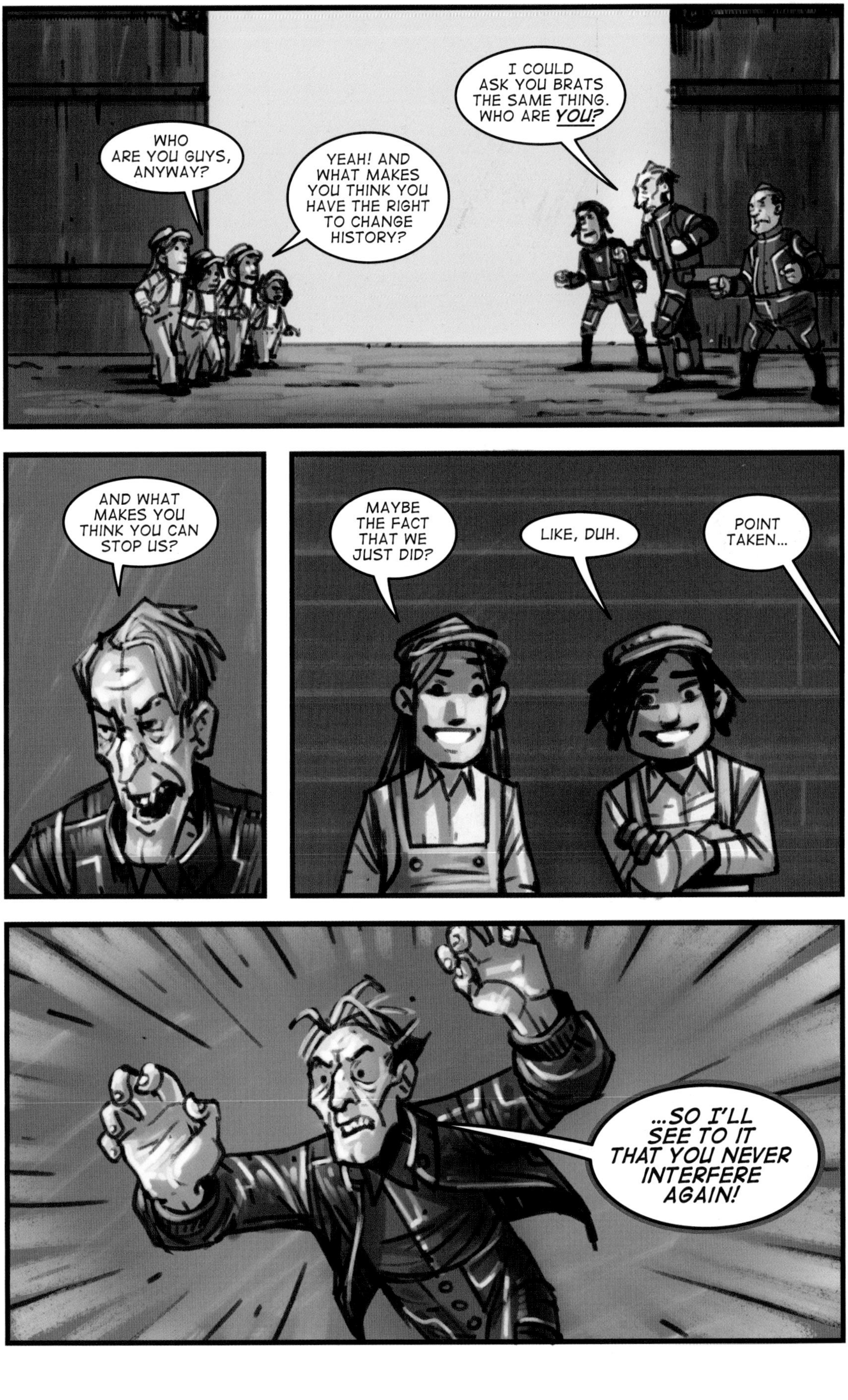
WHO ARE YOU GUYS, ANYWAY?
YEAH! AND WHAT MAKES YOU THINK YOU HAVE THE RIGHT TO CHANGE HISTORY?
I COULD ASK YOU BRATS THE SAME THING. WHO ARE YOU?
AND WHAT MAKES YOU THINK YOU CAN STOP US?
MAYBE THE FACT THAT WE JUST DID?
LIKE, DUH.
POINT TAKEN...
...SO I'LL SEE TO IT THAT YOU NEVER INTERFERE AGAIN!

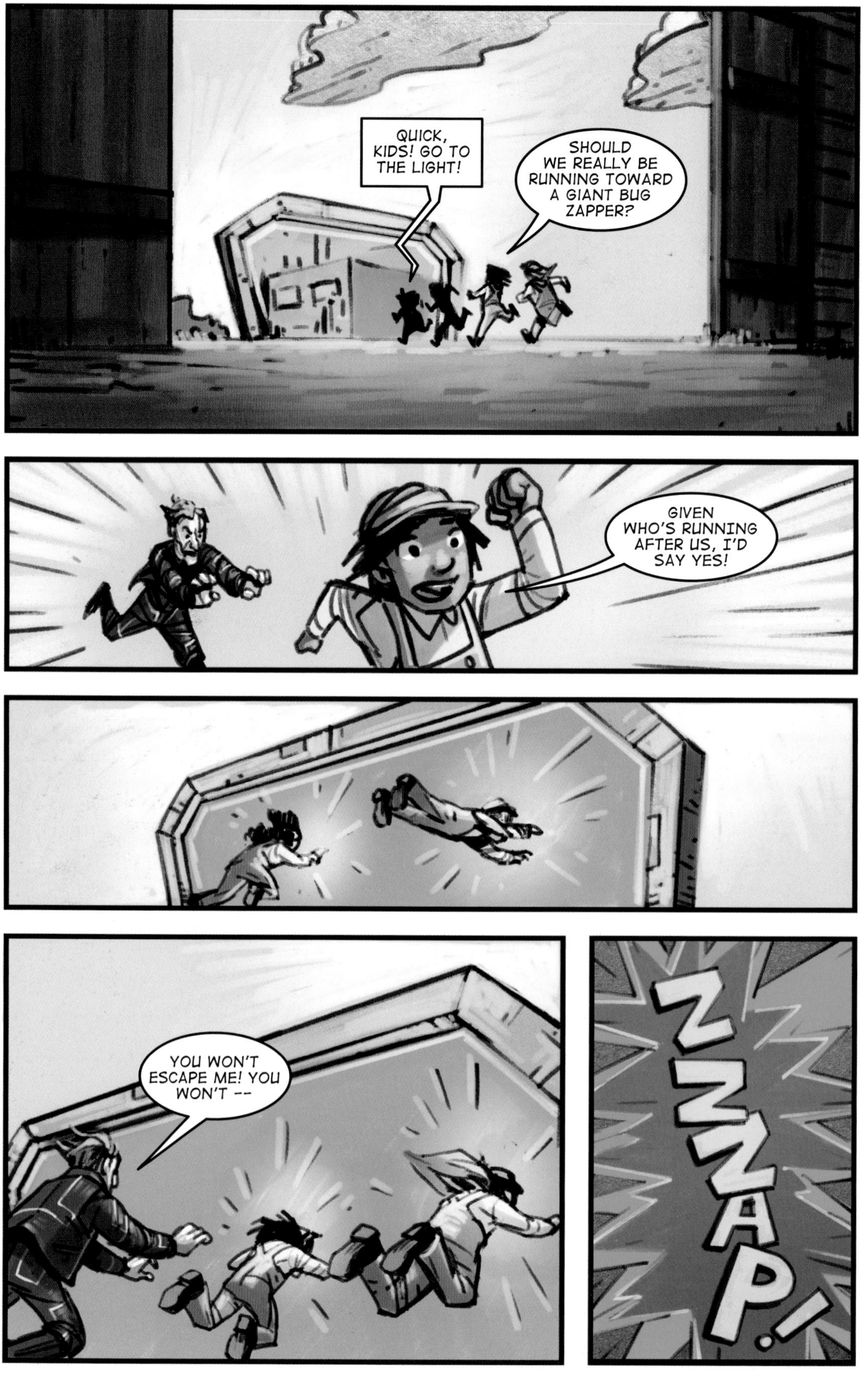
QUICK, KIDS! GO TO THE LIGHT!
SHOULD WE REALLY BE RUNNING TOWARD A GIANT BUG ZAPPER?
GIVEN WHO'S RUNNING AFTER US, I'D SAY YES!
YOU WON'T ESCAPE ME! YOU WON'T --
ZZZAP!

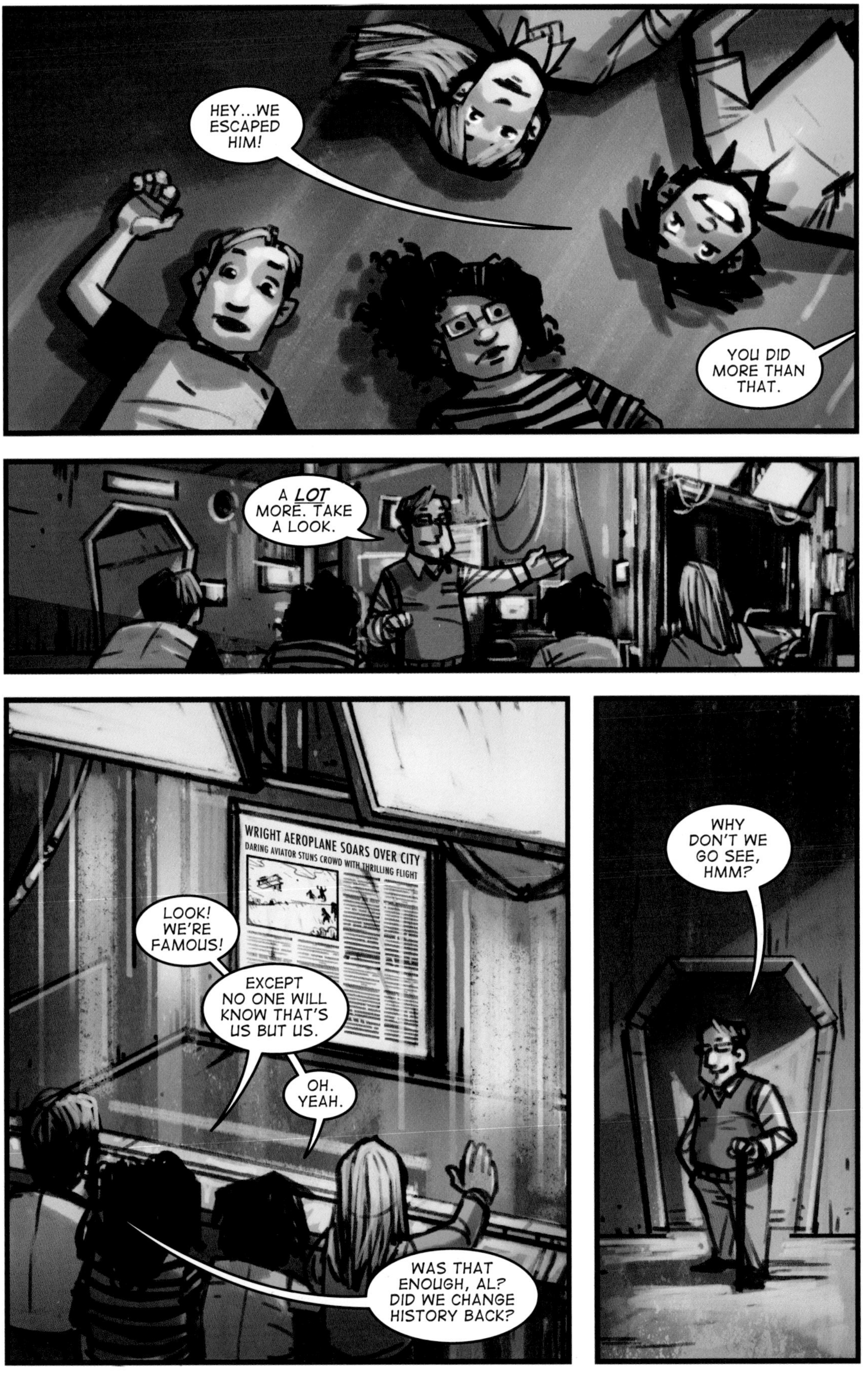
HEY...WE ESCAPED HIM!
YOU DID MORE THAN THAT.
A LOT MORE. TAKE A LOOK.
WRIGHT AEROPLANE SOARS OVER CITY
DARING AVIATOR STUNS CROWD WITH THRILLING FLIGHT
LOOK! WE'RE FAMOUS!
EXCEPT NO ONE WILL KNOW THAT'S US BUT US.
OH. YEAH.
WAS THAT ENOUGH, AL? DID WE CHANGE HISTORY BACK?
WHY DON'T WE GO SEE, HMM?

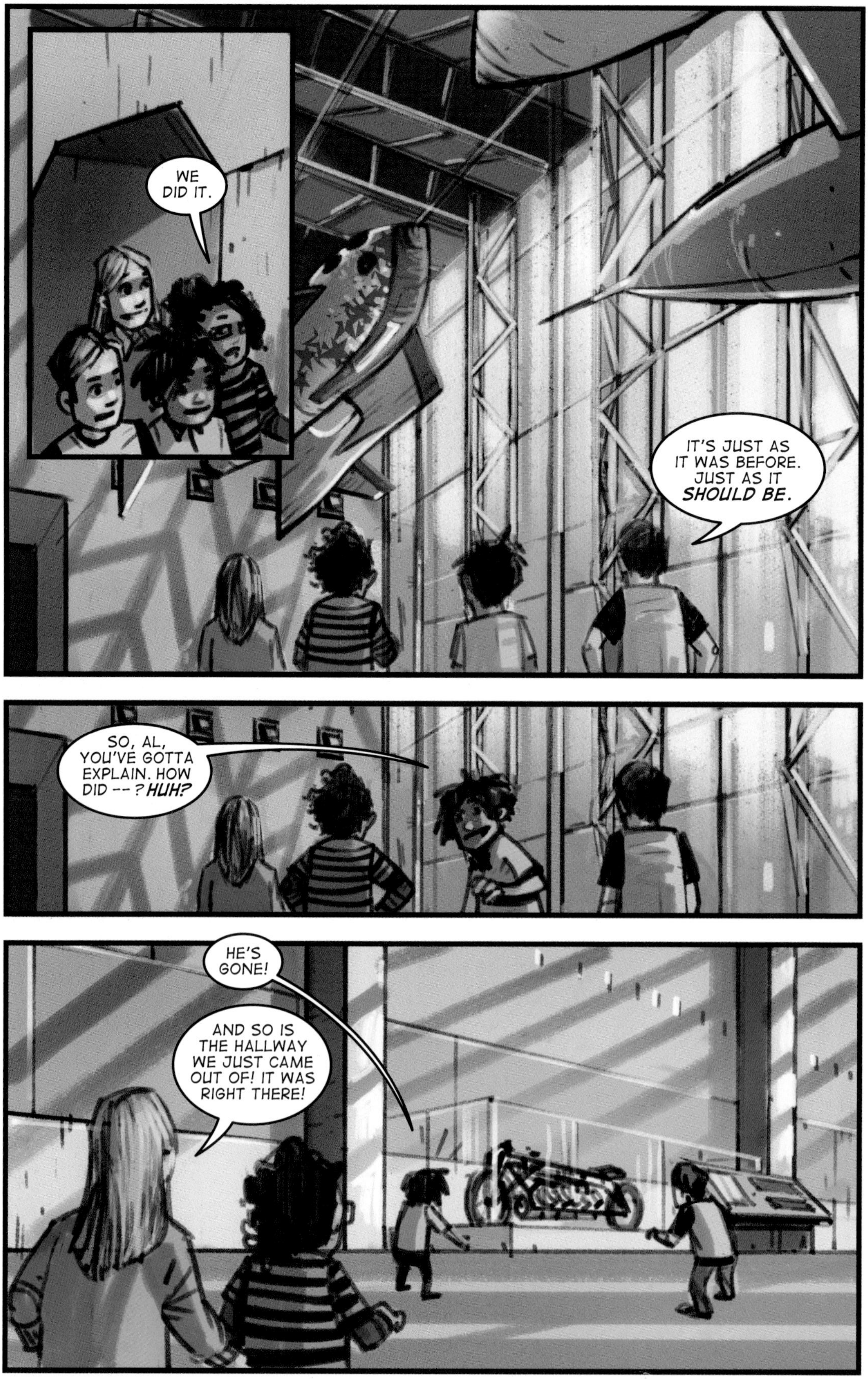
WE DID IT.
IT'S JUST AS IT WAS BEFORE. JUST AS IT *SHOULD BE.*
SO, AL, YOU'VE GOTTA EXPLAIN. HOW DID -- ? *HUH?*
HE'S GONE!
AND SO IS THE HALLWAY WE JUST CAME OUT OF! IT WAS RIGHT THERE!

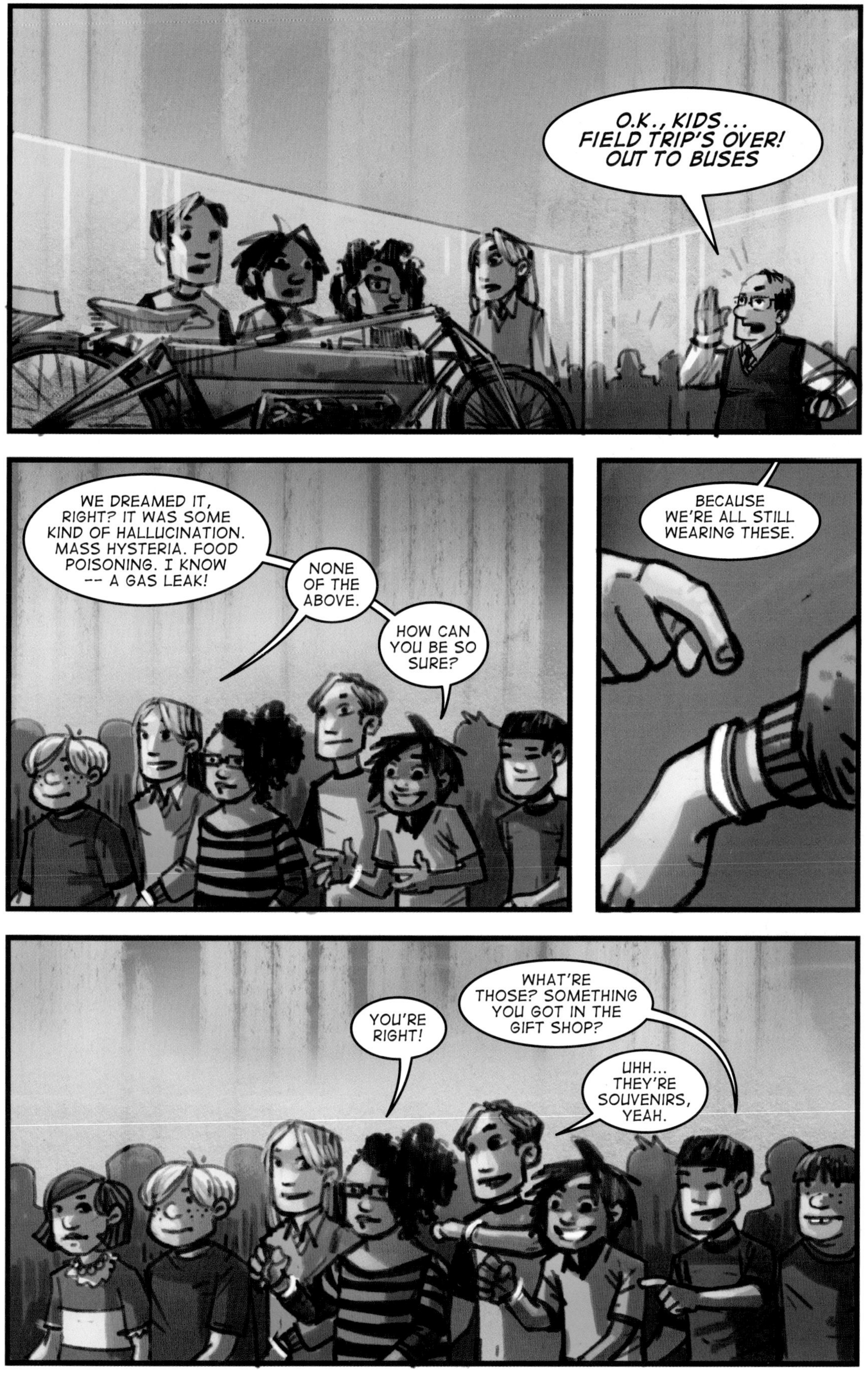
O.K., KIDS... FIELD TRIP'S OVER! OUT TO BUSES
WE DREAMED IT, RIGHT? IT WAS SOME KIND OF HALLUCINATION. MASS HYSTERIA. FOOD POISONING. I KNOW -- A GAS LEAK!
NONE OF THE ABOVE.
HOW CAN YOU BE SO SURE?
BECAUSE WE'RE ALL STILL WEARING THESE.
YOU'RE RIGHT!
WHAT'RE THOSE? SOMETHING YOU GOT IN THE GIFT SHOP?
UHH... THEY'RE SOUVENIRS, YEAH.

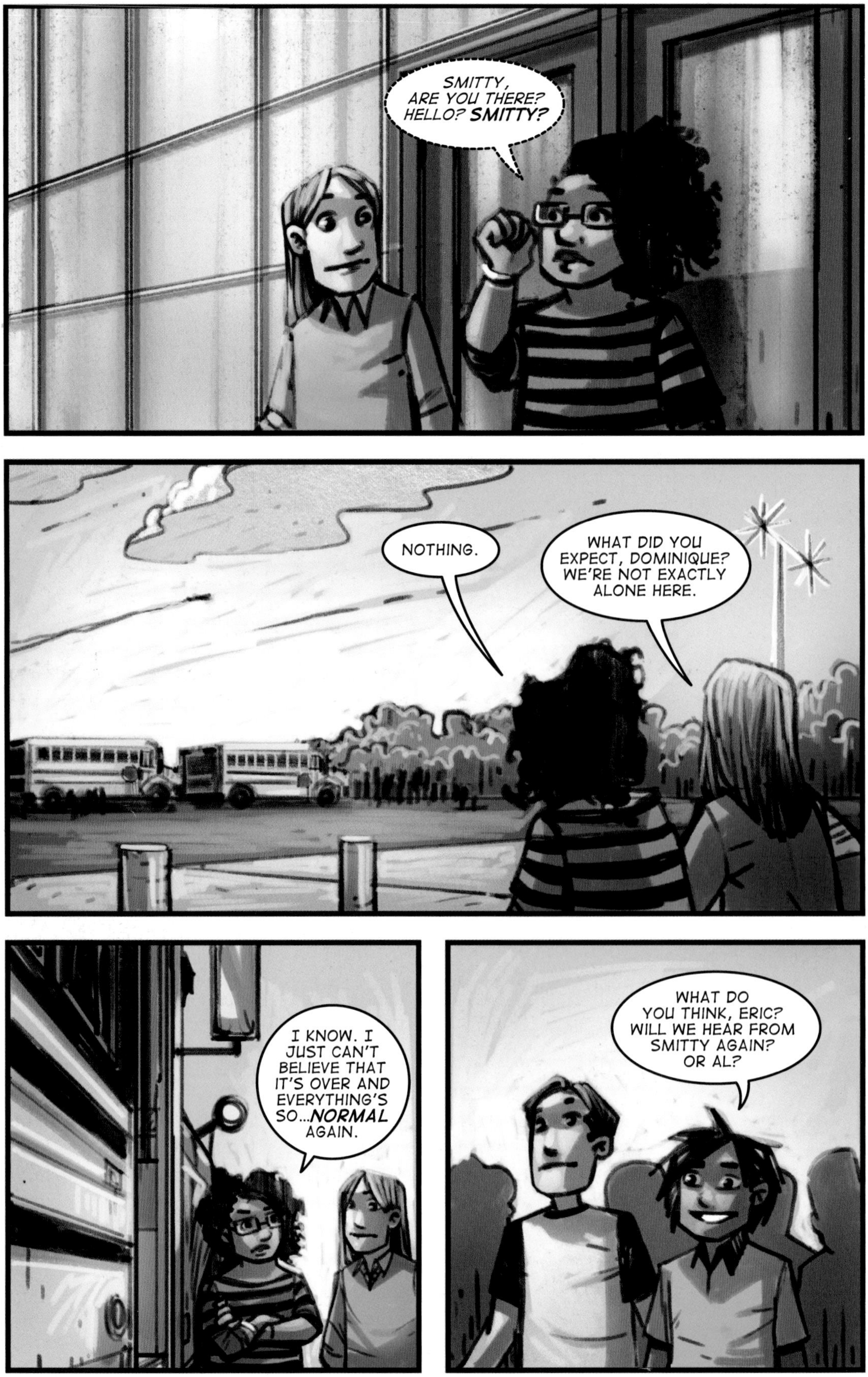
SMITTY, ARE YOU THERE? HELLO? SMITTY?
NOTHING.
WHAT DID YOU EXPECT, DOMINIQUE? WE'RE NOT EXACTLY ALONE HERE.
I KNOW. I JUST CAN'T BELIEVE THAT IT'S OVER AND EVERYTHING'S SO...NORMAL AGAIN.
WHAT DO YOU THINK, ERIC? WILL WE HEAR FROM SMITTY AGAIN? OR AL?

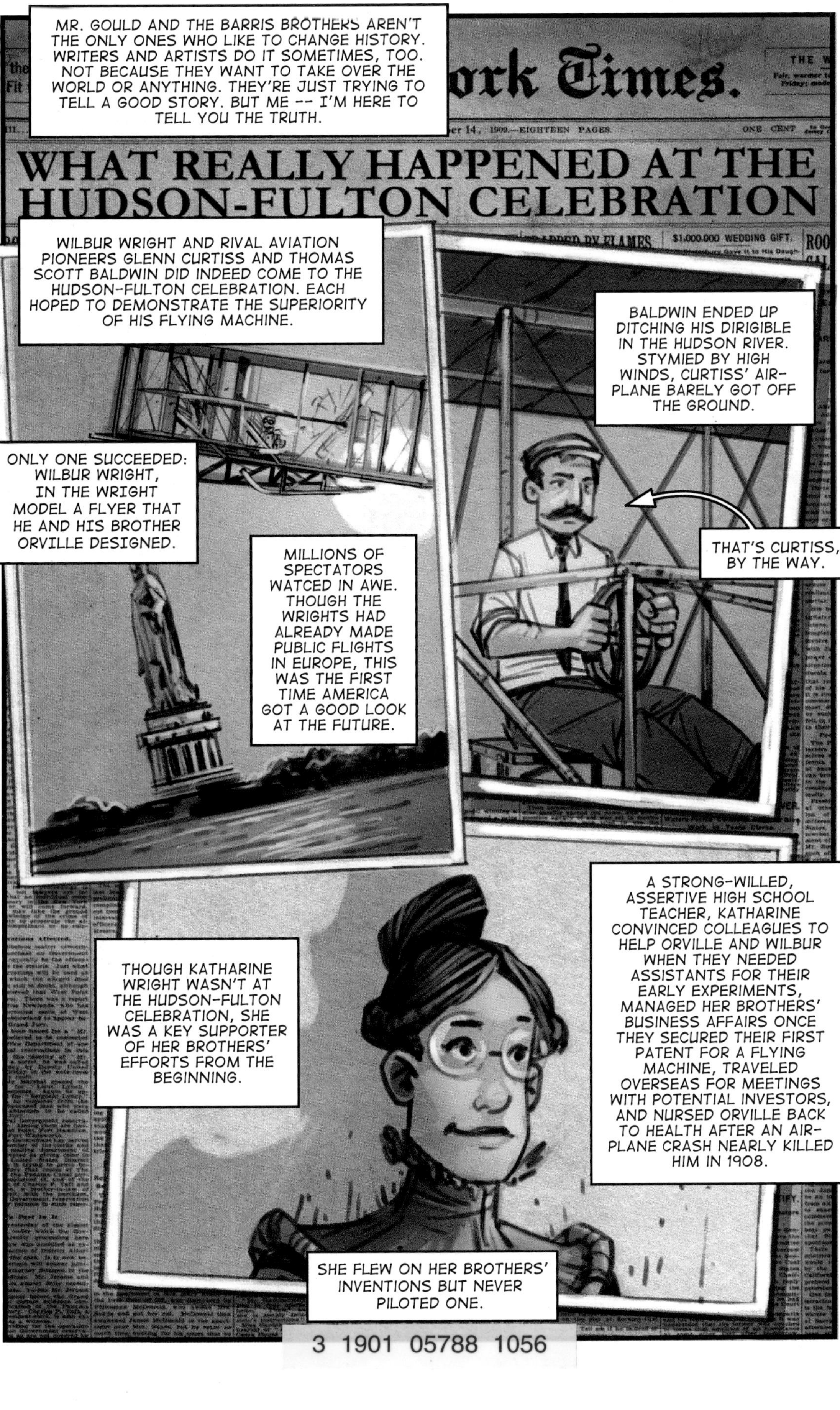
MR. GOULD AND THE BARRIS BROTHERS AREN'T THE ONLY ONES WHO LIKE TO CHANGE HISTORY. WRITERS AND ARTISTS DO IT SOMETIMES, TOO. NOT BECAUSE THEY WANT TO TAKE OVER THE WORLD OR ANYTHING. THEY'RE JUST TRYING TO TELL A GOOD STORY. BUT ME -- I'M HERE TO TELL YOU THE TRUTH.
WHAT REALLY HAPPENED AT THE HUDSON-FULTON CELEBRATION
WILBUR WRIGHT AND RIVAL AVIATION PIONEERS GLENN CURTISS AND THOMAS SCOTT BALDWIN DID INDEED COME TO THE HUDSON-FULTON CELEBRATION. EACH HOPED TO DEMONSTRATE THE SUPERIORITY OF HIS FLYING MACHINE.
ONLY ONE SUCCEEDED: WILBUR WRIGHT, IN THE WRIGHT MODEL A FLYER THAT HE AND HIS BROTHER ORVILLE DESIGNED.
MILLIONS OF SPECTATORS WATCED IN AWE. THOUGH THE WRIGHTS HAD ALREADY MADE PUBLIC FLIGHTS IN EUROPE, THIS WAS THE FIRST TIME AMERICA GOT A GOOD LOOK AT THE FUTURE.
BALDWIN ENDED UP DITCHING HIS DIRIGIBLE IN THE HUDSON RIVER. STYMIED BY HIGH WINDS, CURTISS' AIR-PLANE BARELY GOT OFF THE GROUND.
THAT'S CURTISS, BY THE WAY.
THOUGH KATHARINE WRIGHT WASN'T AT THE HUDSON-FULTON CELEBRATION, SHE WAS A KEY SUPPORTER OF HER BROTHERS' EFFORTS FROM THE BEGINNING.
A STRONG-WILLED, ASSERTIVE HIGH SCHOOL TEACHER, KATHARINE CONVINCED COLLEAGUES TO HELP ORVILLE AND WILBUR WHEN THEY NEEDED ASSISTANTS FOR THEIR EARLY EXPERIMENTS, MANAGED HER BROTHERS' BUSINESS AFFAIRS ONCE THEY SECURED THEIR FIRST PATENT FOR A FLYING MACHINE, TRAVELED OVERSEAS FOR MEETINGS WITH POTENTIAL INVESTORS, AND NURSED ORVILLE BACK TO HEALTH AFTER AN AIR-PLANE CRASH NEARLY KILLED HIM IN 1908.
SHE FLEW ON HER BROTHERS' INVENTIONS BUT NEVER PILOTED ONE.

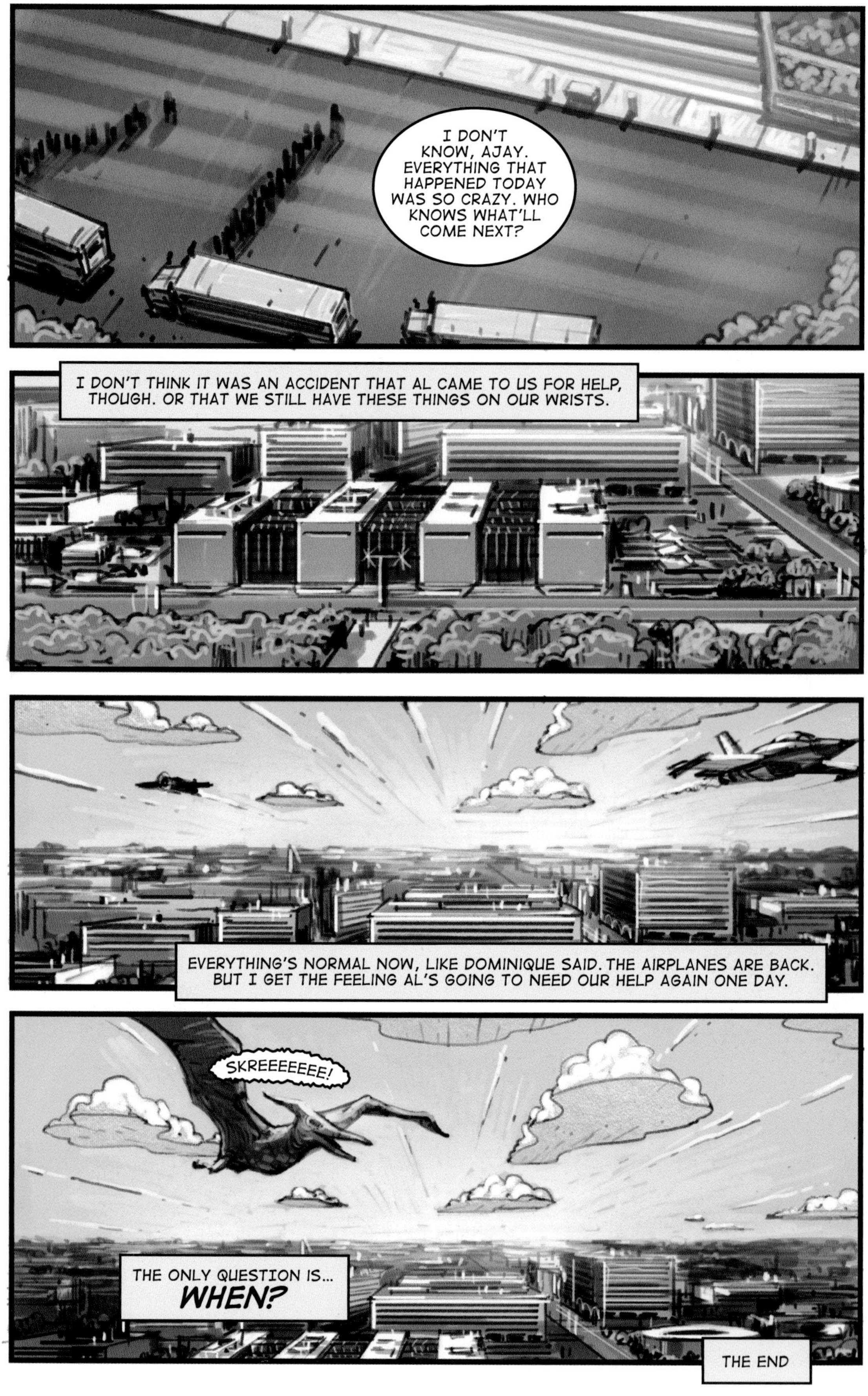
I DON'T KNOW, AJAY. EVERYTHING THAT HAPPENED TODAY WAS SO CRAZY. WHO KNOWS WHAT'LL COME NEXT?
I DON'T THINK IT WAS AN ACCIDENT THAT AL CAME TO US FOR HELP, THOUGH. OR THAT WE STILL HAVE THESE THINGS ON OUR WRISTS.
EVERYTHING'S NORMAL NOW, LIKE DOMINIQUE SAID. THE AIRPLANES ARE BACK. BUT I GET THE FEELING AL'S GOING TO NEED OUR HELP AGAIN ONE DAY.
SKREEEEEEE!
THE ONLY QUESTION IS... *WHEN?*
THE END